PREFACE

The field of Object-Oriented Analysis and Design (OOAD) is pivotal in the world of software engineering and development, as it equips students and professionals with the tools and methodologies to conceptualize, design, and implement complex software systems effectively. The IGNOU MCS-219 course on OOAD is designed to provide students with a robust understanding of the principles and practices that underlie object-oriented software design. This course serves as a cornerstone for those pursuing a career in software development, as it lays the foundation for mastering the art of designing systems that are modular, maintainable, and scalable.

This book, 'IGNOU MCS-219 Object-Oriented Analysis and Design Previous Years Unsolved Papers', has been meticulously compiled to serve as a comprehensive resource for students preparing for their examinations in this critical subject. The unsolved papers included in this book have been selected from previous years' question papers, offering a wide range of problems that reflect the diversity and depth of the subject matter covered in the MCS-219 course. These papers provide students with an invaluable opportunity to test their understanding, apply theoretical knowledge, and refine their problem-solving skills in the context of object-oriented design. This book is not only a study aid but also a tool for self-assessment and continuous learning. It encourages students to think critically and analytically, to approach problems with a structured mindset, and to explore multiple solutions to complex design scenarios. For educators, this book offers a rich repository of exam-style questions that can be used to create practice tests, assignments, or classroom discussions.

IGNOU MCS-219 Object-Oriented Analysis and Design Previous Years Unsolved Papers is an essential resource for any student aiming to master the intricacies of object-oriented design. It is our hope that this book will serve as a catalyst for deeper learning and a springboard for academic and professional success in the ever-evolving field of software engineering. Whether you are a student preparing for exams, an educator seeking quality material, or a professional revisiting foundational concept, this book is designed to meet your needs and support your journey in the world of Object-Oriented Analysis and Design.

Table of Contents

MCS – 219

Master Of Computer Applications (MCA)
Chapter 1: Term-End Examination, December, 2021
MCS-219: Object-Oriented Analysis and Design

Time: 3 Hours
Maximum Marks: 100

Note: (i) Question No. 1 is compulsory.
(ii) Attempt any three Questions from the rest.

1.(a) What is object-oriented analysis and design? Explain its advantages. 10

(b)What is Association? What are the different types of association? Explain with the help of an example of each. 10

(c)What is Object Model? Explain the use of object model in "software system development "with the help of an example. 10

(d)What is activity diagram? Explain its purpose with the help of an example. 10

2.(a) What is DFD? Briefly explain the symbols used in DFD. Draw DFD up to level 1 for "Online Library System". Make necessary assumptions. 12

(b)Explain the concepts of abstraction and encapsulation with the help of an example for each. 8

3.(a)What is use case diagram? Draw use case diagram for ATM cash withdrawal process. 10

(b)An online library system provides facility for online membership on payment of subscription fee. This system provides facility of access and downloading the books and research articles. Draw class diagram for this system. Make necessary assumptions. 10

4.(a)Explain mapping of ternary associations to database tables with the help of an example. 10

(b)Explain dynamic modelling with the help of an example and a suitable diagram. 10

5.Write short notes on the following: $4\times5=20$
(a)Object ID and its advantages
(b)Collaboration diagram
(c)Design optimization
(d)Features of a good object design

MCS – 219

Master Of Computer Applications (MCA)
Chapter 2: Term-End Examination, June, 2022
MCS-219: Object-Oriented Analysis and Design

Time: 3 Hours
Maximum Marks: 100

Note: (i) Question No. 1 is compulsory.
(ii) Attempt any three Questions from the rest.

1. (a) What is object orientation? Explain the principles of object orientation. Also list the advantages of object orientation. 10

(b) What is generalization? How is it different from specialization? Explain with the help of an example and diagram. 10

(c) What is UML? Explain the advantages of using UML. Draw a use case diagram for book issue and return in a library system. Make necessary assumptions. 10

(d) What is association? Explain the advantages of two-way association over one-way association, with the help of an example. 10

2. (a) What is a class diagram? Draw a class diagram for ''Online Banking System''. Make necessary assumptions. 10

(b) What is DFD? List the symbols used in DFD. Draw up to level 1 DFD for an ''Online Banking System''. Make necessary assumptions. 10

3. (a) What is a dynamic model? Explain any two UML diagrams used in dynamic modelling. 10

(b) Explain how classes of a system are mapped to database tables, with the help of a suitable example and diagram. 10

4. (a) Explain the concept of inheritance and polymorphism in OOAD, with the help of examples. 10

(b) What is aggregation? Why is it called a special kind of association? Explain with the help of an example. 10

5. Write short notes on the following: 4 X 5=20
(a) State Diagram
(b) Object Design
(c) Implementing Association
(d) Integrity Constraints

MCS – 219

Master Of Computer Applications (MCA)
Chapter 3: Term-End Examination, December, 2022
MCS-219: Object-Oriented Analysis and Design

Time: 3 Hours
Maximum Marks: 100

Note: (i) Question No. 1 is compulsory.
(ii) Attempt any three Questions from the rest.

1. (a) An online banking facility allows customers to check their balances and perform online transactions for purchase of goods. A customer should have an account with the bank in order to use this facility. Draw a class diagram for this system. Make necessary assumptions. 10

(b) What is an event? Explain with the help of an example. Also define the term scenario in this context. What is a state? How is it related to an event? Why do you draw a state chart diagram? Explain the symbols used in state chart diagram with the help of an example diagram. 10

(c) Explain the factors that impact the choice of algorithm in the context of object design. What are the tasks of designer while performing design optimisation? Explain each task with the help of an example. 10

(d) How can you map object classes to tables? Explain with the help of an example. Also explain how you map one-to-many association to tables, with the help of an example. 10

2. (a) What are the objectives of use-case diagram? Draw a use-case diagram for book issue and return system in a library. Make suitable assumptions. How are interaction diagram different for use case diagrams? 10

(b) What is the purpose of drawing component diagram? Explain the graphical components that are used to draw a component diagram. Draw and explain component diagram of ATM system. Make suitable assumptions. 10

3. (a) Explain the symbols that are used to draw a DFD. Draw and explain 1st level DFD for online shopping system. List any six limitations of DFDs. 10

(b) Explain how large system can be decomposed into sub-systems using horizontal or vertical partition with the help of an example. 10

4. (a) A university has post-graduate and undergraduate students. The post-graduate students can be research scholars or master degree students. The research scholar's can be scholarship holder and without any scholarship. The postgraduate and under-graduate students can be hostlers (who stay in hostel) or day scholar (who do not stay in hostels). Draw the generalisation hierarchy of the student class. 5

(b) What are abstract classes? How can they be related to concrete classes? Explain with the help of an example. 5

(c) Draw an activity diagram for making an online banking transaction. Make suitable assumptions. 5

(d) What is the significance of a good design documentation? What should be the contents of a good design document? 5

5. Explain the following with the help of an example: 4×5=20
(a) Implementation of one-to-one unidirectional association
(b) Persistency of data, process and object
(c) Extended three schema architecture for object model
(d) Collaboration diagram

MCS – 219

Master Of Computer Applications (MCA)
Chapter 4: Term-End Examination, June, 2023
MCS-219: Object-Oriented Analysis and Design

Time: 3 Hours
Maximum Marks: 100

Note: (i) Question No. 1 is compulsory.
(ii) Attempt any three Questions from the rest.

1. (a) An online admission system of a University provides facility to its prospective learner to apply for various UG and PG courses. During the application process applicants need to provide their basic details such as name, date of birth, mobile number, emailid and address. Also they need to upload their certificates for which system provides proper instructions and interfaces. Subsequent upon processing the applications received, university displays the list of selected candidates and also send them email regarding their selection. Applicants pay the fee online and their id cards are generated. Draw the following diagrams for this system. (You can make necessary assumptions, if required):
(i) Use case diagram 5
(ii) Class diagram 5
(iii) Sequence diagram 5
(iv) State diagram 5

(b) What is DFD? Draw upto level 1 DFD for the system described in Q1(a) above. 10

(c) What is generalization? Explain how generalization is different from aggregation with the help of class diagram for "Computer System". 10

2. (a) Explain the concepts of links and association with the help of example. Also, discuss how associations are implemented. 10

(b) What is activity diagram? Draw activity diagram for online shopping of mobile charger. 10

3. (a) What is deployment diagram? What are components of deployment diagram? Draw deployment diagram for "Online Admission System of a University". 10

(b) What is object diagram? Draw and explain object diagram for Saving Accounts in a Bank. 10

4. (a) What is concurrency control? Explain need of concurrency control in a system with the help of an example. 10

(b) Explain need of inheritance adjustment in designing of a system with the help of an example. 10

5. Write short notes on the following: 4×5=20
(a) Use of object ID
(b) Design Documentation
(c) Meta Data and Keys
(d) Basic philosophy of object orientation

MCS – 219

Master Of Computer Applications (MCA)
Chapter 5: Term-End Examination, December, 2023
MCS-219: Object-Oriented Analysis and Design

Time: 3 Hours
Maximum Marks: 100

Note: (i) Question No. 1 is compulsory.
(ii) Attempt any three Questions from the rest.

1. (a) "Object Oriented Analysis and Design is better than Structured Analysis and Design." Explain in detail. Justify the above statement. 10

(b) What is UML? What are its advantages? Draw class diagram for an ATM system. 10

(c) What is inheritance? Explain advantages of inheritance. 5

(d) What is an association? Explain use of link in representation of association with the help of a diagram. 5

(e) What is design documentation? Briefly explain the features of a good design documentation. 5

(f) What is a functional model? Which diagram is used in functional modeling? Explain in brief. 5

2. (a) What is State Transition Diagram? Draw State Transition Diagram for an ATM machine/system. 10

(b) What is Generalization? How is it different from Specialization? Explain with an example using suitable UML diagrams. 10

3. (a) What is a constraint? Explain how constraints are shown in a class diagram. 5

(b) What is serialization? Explain its use. 5

(c) Explain the difference between unidirectional and bidirectional association. Describe how bidirectional association is implemented. 10

4. (a) What is a component diagram? What are its advantages? Draw component diagram for ATM system. 10

(b) What is Aggregation? Explain the use of aggregation in object oriented system design with the help of an example. 10

5. Write short notes on the following: 4×5=20
(a) Abstract class
(b) Use case Diagram
(c) Sequence Diagram
(d) Object Class and Database Tables

Chapter 6: Most Asked Questions Part-A

1. What is object-oriented analysis and design, and why is it important in software development?
Answer: Object-oriented analysis and design (OOAD) is a methodology that focuses on analyzing and designing a system using the concepts of objects and classes. It emphasizes encapsulation, inheritance, and polymorphism to create reusable and maintainable software components. OOAD bridges the gap between user requirements and technical implementation by modeling real-world entities and their interactions. This approach is crucial for developing complex, large-scale systems as it promotes modularity, scalability, and easier maintenance. By aligning design closely with user needs and system behavior, OOAD helps developers create robust and adaptable software solutions that evolve with changing business requirements.

2. Explain the differences between object-oriented analysis (OOA) and object-oriented design (OOD).
Answer: Object-oriented analysis (OOA) focuses on understanding and modeling user requirements by identifying the objects, classes, and relationships in a system without considering implementation details. It answers "what" the system must do. In contrast, object-oriented design (OOD) translates these requirements into a detailed blueprint for building the system, defining how objects will interact, what methods they will have, and how data will flow. OOD addresses the "how" aspect of system creation. While OOA emphasizes conceptual modeling, OOD bridges the conceptual and technical worlds, providing a foundation for implementing software effectively using object-oriented programming languages.

3. What are the key principles of object-oriented design?
Answer: The key principles of object-oriented design include encapsulation, abstraction, inheritance, and polymorphism. Encapsulation hides internal details and exposes only necessary interfaces, promoting modularity. Abstraction simplifies complex systems by focusing on essential features. Inheritance allows classes to reuse and extend functionality from parent classes, fostering code reuse. Polymorphism enables objects to take multiple forms, allowing dynamic method binding and flexibility. Additional principles like low coupling and high cohesion ensure that components interact minimally and focus on single responsibilities. Together, these principles create systems that are easier to maintain, extend, and adapt to future changes in requirements.

4. Define encapsulation and explain its role in object-oriented systems.
Answer: Encapsulation is the object-oriented principle of bundling data (attributes) and methods (functions) that operate on the data within a single unit called a class. It restricts direct access to some of an object's components by using access modifiers like private, protected, and public. Encapsulation's primary role is to enforce information hiding, ensuring that internal details are shielded from external interference and misuse. This promotes modularity and maintainability by allowing developers to modify internal implementations without affecting other parts of the system. Encapsulation also enhances security, as only controlled interactions with data are permitted through defined interfaces.

5. What is inheritance in OOAD, and how does it promote code reuse?
Answer: Inheritance is an object-oriented feature that allows a class (child or subclass) to inherit attributes and methods from another class (parent or superclass). It enables developers to define common behaviors in a base class and reuse them in derived classes, reducing code duplication. Inheritance promotes extensibility, as new functionalities can be added to subclasses without altering existing code. For example, a base class "Vehicle" may define generic methods like start() and stop(), which can be inherited by subclasses like "Car" and "Bike." This hierarchy improves maintainability, scalability, and logical organization in software systems.

6. Differentiate between class diagrams and sequence diagrams in UML.
Answer: Class diagrams and sequence diagrams are two distinct types of UML diagrams serving different purposes in OOAD. Class diagrams represent the static structure of a system by depicting classes, their attributes, methods, and relationships like inheritance, association, and dependency. They provide a blueprint of the system's architecture. Sequence diagrams, on the other hand, illustrate dynamic behavior by showing how objects interact over time. They detail the sequence of messages exchanged between objects to complete a specific function or scenario. While class diagrams focus on structure, sequence diagrams emphasize communication and flow of operations.

7. Explain polymorphism with an example in object-oriented systems.
Answer: Polymorphism allows objects of different classes to be treated as objects of a common parent class, enabling a single interface to represent multiple types. It comes in two forms: compile-time (method overloading) and runtime (method overriding). For example, consider a base class "Shape" with a method draw(). Subclasses like "Circle" and "Rectangle" override draw() to provide specific implementations. A program can call draw() on a Shape reference, and at runtime, the appropriate method is invoked based on the actual object type. Polymorphism enhances flexibility, allowing developers to write generic and reusable code that adapts to various scenarios.

8. What is aggregation in OOAD, and how does it differ from composition?
Answer: Aggregation and composition are two types of relationships between objects in OOAD that depict "has-a" associations. Aggregation represents a weaker relationship where the child can exist independently of the parent. For example, a "Department" may aggregate multiple "Employee" objects, but employees can still exist without the department. Composition, however, depicts a strong relationship where the child cannot exist without the parent. For instance, a "House" composed of "Rooms" means if the house is destroyed, the rooms cease to exist. Aggregation suggests shared ownership, while composition implies exclusive ownership and tighter coupling.

9. How does OOAD improve software maintainability?
Answer: OOAD improves software maintainability by emphasizing modular, reusable, and loosely coupled components. Encapsulation hides internal details, reducing the impact of changes on other parts of the system. Inheritance allows new features to be added without altering existing code, while polymorphism supports flexible, extendable designs. The use of UML diagrams and models helps developers understand system behavior and relationships, facilitating easier debugging and updates. OOAD also encourages high cohesion within classes and low coupling between them, ensuring that changes in one module have minimal ripple effects, resulting in robust and easily maintainable software solutions.

10. What are use case diagrams in UML, and why are they important?
Answer: Use case diagrams in UML model the functional requirements of a system by illustrating interactions between external actors (users or other systems) and the system's use cases (functionalities). They provide a high-level view of what the system should do without detailing implementation specifics. Use case diagrams are important because they help stakeholders visualize requirements, identify system boundaries, and prioritize features during analysis. They serve as a communication bridge between technical teams and non-technical stakeholders, ensuring a shared understanding of system goals and user interactions in object-oriented analysis and design processes.

11. What is object-oriented modeling, and how is it used in software development?
Answer: Object-oriented modeling (OOM) is the process of visually representing the structure and behavior of a system using object-oriented concepts like classes, objects, inheritance, and relationships. It serves as a blueprint for software development, helping developers understand the system's components and interactions before coding. Tools like UML diagrams support this modeling process, providing static views (e.g., class diagrams) and dynamic views (e.g., sequence diagrams). OOM bridges the gap between requirements and implementation by aligning designs with real-world entities. It simplifies communication among stakeholders, supports reuse of components, and ensures that software systems are scalable and maintainable.

12. Explain the concept of abstraction in OOAD with an example.
Answer: Abstraction in OOAD involves simplifying complex systems by focusing on essential details and ignoring irrelevant ones. It allows developers to model real-world entities by defining only the necessary attributes and behaviors. For example, in a "Car" class, attributes like speed, fuel level, and methods like start() and stop() are included, while manufacturing details are abstracted away. Abstraction helps manage complexity and promotes reusable, adaptable designs. It also supports the creation of interfaces and abstract classes, which define contracts for subclasses to implement specific behaviors, ensuring consistency across the system.

13. What is a class in object-oriented programming, and how does it differ from an object?
Answer: A class is a blueprint or template that defines the properties (attributes) and behaviors (methods) common to all objects of a particular type. An object, on the other hand, is an instance of a class created at runtime. For example, a "Car" class defines properties like color and engine type, while an object like "myCar" represents a specific car with a red color and V6 engine. Classes define structure and behavior, while objects represent actual entities in memory.

This distinction is central to object-oriented programming, enabling the creation of multiple unique instances from a single design.

14. How does OOAD support modularity in software systems?
Answer: OOAD supports modularity by organizing software into discrete, self-contained units called classes and objects, each responsible for specific functionality. Encapsulation ensures that internal details are hidden, allowing components to interact only through well-defined interfaces. Inheritance and polymorphism further promote modular design by enabling code reuse and flexible extensions without altering existing modules. This modular approach simplifies development, testing, and maintenance, as changes to one module have minimal impact on others. OOAD's focus on modularity enhances collaboration among development teams and supports the creation of scalable, robust software systems.

15. What is the difference between association, aggregation, and composition in UML?
Answer: In UML, association, aggregation, and composition represent relationships between classes but differ in strength and dependency. Association indicates a general connection where objects may or may not depend on each other, such as a "Teacher" associated with a "Student." Aggregation represents a "has-a" relationship with shared ownership, where child objects can exist independently of the parent (e.g., "Library" and "Books"). Composition is a stronger form of aggregation where child objects depend on the parent for their lifecycle (e.g., "House" and "Rooms"). Composition implies exclusive ownership and tighter coupling compared to aggregation.

16. Explain the concept of dynamic binding in object-oriented programming.
Answer: Dynamic binding, also known as late binding, refers to the process of resolving method calls at runtime rather than compile time. It enables polymorphism by allowing a program to determine which method implementation to execute based on the actual object type. For example, if a base class reference points to a derived class object, the overridden method in the derived class is invoked at runtime. Dynamic binding promotes flexibility and extensibility in software design, allowing developers to write generic code that adapts dynamically to specific object behaviors during program execution.

17. What is the role of UML in object-oriented analysis and design?
Answer: Unified Modeling Language (UML) is a standardized visual language used to represent the structure, behavior, and interactions of object-oriented systems. In OOAD, UML provides tools like class diagrams, sequence diagrams, and use case diagrams to model requirements, design architecture, and visualize workflows. UML facilitates communication between developers, analysts, and stakeholders by providing a common representation of system components and relationships. Its role extends from conceptual modeling in analysis to detailed design specifications, ensuring clarity, consistency, and traceability throughout the software development lifecycle.

18. How does inheritance promote extensibility in software design?
Answer: Inheritance promotes extensibility by allowing new classes (subclasses) to build upon existing ones (superclasses) without rewriting code. Developers can add or override functionalities in subclasses while retaining the shared attributes and methods of the parent class. This mechanism enables the creation of hierarchical structures where general behaviors are defined at higher levels and specialized behaviors at lower levels. For instance, a "Vehicle" superclass can be extended into "Car" and "Bike" subclasses with additional features. Inheritance streamlines code reuse, supports incremental enhancements, and simplifies the integration of new functionalities in evolving software systems.

19. Explain the concept of method overloading and method overriding in OOAD.
Answer: Method overloading and method overriding are techniques to achieve polymorphism in OOAD. Method overloading occurs when multiple methods in the same class share the same name but differ in parameter lists (type or number). It is resolved at compile time (static polymorphism). Method overriding happens when a subclass provides a specific implementation of a method defined in its superclass. It requires the method signature to be the same and is resolved at runtime (dynamic polymorphism). Overloading enhances flexibility within a class, while overriding allows subclasses to customize inherited behaviors.

20. What are the benefits of using object-oriented design patterns?
Answer: Object-oriented design patterns provide proven solutions to common software design problems, promoting best practices and standardization in development. Benefits include improved code reuse, reduced development time, and enhanced system flexibility. Patterns like Singleton, Observer, and Factory simplify complex designs by offering clear guidelines for implementation. They facilitate communication among developers by providing a shared vocabulary for recurring challenges. Design patterns also improve maintainability by encouraging modular, loosely coupled architectures. By leveraging these patterns, developers can create scalable, robust, and adaptable software systems that meet evolving requirements effectively.

21. Explain the concept of state diagrams in UML and their use in OOAD.
Answer: State diagrams in UML model the dynamic behavior of a system by illustrating the possible states an object can occupy and the transitions triggered by events. Each state represents a specific condition or situation, while transitions depict how the object responds to inputs. In OOAD, state diagrams are used to analyze and design systems where objects undergo significant state changes, such as ATM operations or traffic light control. They help developers understand system workflows, ensure proper handling of events, and design robust software that reacts predictably to various scenarios.

22. What is the difference between static and dynamic modeling in OOAD?
Answer: Static modeling focuses on representing the structural aspects of a system, such as classes, objects, attributes, and their relationships. It provides a blueprint of the system's architecture using diagrams like class and object diagrams. Dynamic modeling, on the other hand, emphasizes the behavioral aspects, including interactions, state changes, and message flows among objects over time. Sequence diagrams, activity diagrams, and state diagrams are examples of dynamic models. While static modeling captures the system's "what," dynamic modeling captures the "how," ensuring a comprehensive understanding of both structure and behavior in OOAD.

23. How does polymorphism improve flexibility in software systems?
Answer: Polymorphism improves flexibility by allowing a single interface to handle different underlying object types, enabling developers to write generic and reusable code. For instance, a function designed to process a "Shape" object can operate on "Circle," "Rectangle," or "Triangle" objects without modification. This reduces code duplication and simplifies system extensions. Runtime polymorphism, achieved through method overriding, supports dynamic behavior adjustments, while compile-time polymorphism, via method overloading, offers multiple ways to perform similar tasks. Polymorphism enhances adaptability, maintainability, and scalability in software systems, aligning with the key principles of object-oriented design.

24. What are the advantages of low coupling and high cohesion in OOAD?
Answer: Low coupling and high cohesion are essential principles in OOAD that promote maintainable and robust software systems. Low coupling ensures minimal interdependencies between classes or modules, allowing them to function independently and reducing the impact of changes. High cohesion means each class or module focuses on a single responsibility, enhancing clarity and reusability. Together, they improve modularity, simplify testing, and facilitate parallel development by teams. Systems designed with low coupling and high cohesion are easier to extend, debug, and maintain, resulting in higher software quality and lower long-term costs.

25. Explain the purpose of component diagrams in OOAD.
Answer: Component diagrams in OOAD model the physical structure of a system by illustrating how software components interact and depend on each other. They depict the organization of executable modules, libraries, and interfaces, showing how different parts of the system are assembled. Component diagrams are crucial during the design and deployment phases, as they provide insights into system architecture, facilitate dependency management, and support modular development. They also help stakeholders visualize how high-level functionality maps to specific components, ensuring a clear understanding of the system's implementation structure.

26. What is the difference between interface and abstract class in object-oriented design?
Answer: In object-oriented design, an interface defines a contract consisting of method signatures without any implementation, while an abstract class can provide both abstract methods (without implementation) and concrete methods (with implementation). Interfaces support multiple inheritances, allowing a class to implement multiple interfaces simultaneously, whereas abstract classes support single inheritance. Interfaces are ideal for defining

completely unimplemented behaviors that multiple classes can adopt, while abstract classes are suited for sharing common code among related classes. The choice between them depends on design requirements, flexibility needs, and programming language capabilities.

27. How do design principles like SOLID apply to OOAD?
Answer: The SOLID design principles enhance OOAD by promoting maintainable, flexible, and scalable software systems. Single Responsibility Principle (SRP) ensures classes focus on one task. Open/Closed Principle (OCP) allows extending functionality without altering existing code. Liskov Substitution Principle (LSP) promotes substitutability of subclasses for parent classes. Interface Segregation Principle (ISP) advises against forcing clients to depend on unused interfaces. Dependency Inversion Principle (DIP) suggests relying on abstractions rather than concrete implementations. Applying SOLID in OOAD leads to loosely coupled, highly cohesive designs that support long-term evolution and minimize technical debt.

28. Explain the concept of object identity in OOAD.
Answer: Object identity in OOAD refers to the unique property that distinguishes one object from another, even if they have identical attribute values. It ensures that each object can be uniquely referenced within a system. For example, two "Car" objects may have the same model and color but are treated as distinct entities due to their unique identities. Object identity is implemented using memory references or unique identifiers (like IDs in databases). This concept is fundamental in object-oriented systems for tracking object states, managing associations, and ensuring data integrity.

29. What is the significance of activity diagrams in OOAD?
Answer: Activity diagrams in OOAD represent the flow of control or data within a system, illustrating how tasks and processes are performed step by step. They are particularly useful for modeling workflows, business processes, and complex operations involving multiple actors or components. Activity diagrams show decision points, parallel flows, and transitions between activities, making them ideal for visualizing dynamic system behaviors. They help developers and stakeholders understand process logic, identify bottlenecks, and design efficient algorithms. Activity diagrams are critical during analysis and design phases to ensure clear and accurate system modeling.

30. How does OOAD help in building scalable software systems?
Answer: OOAD helps in building scalable software systems by emphasizing modular design, reusability, and separation of concerns. Features like inheritance and polymorphism allow developers to extend functionality without disrupting existing components. Encapsulation ensures that system changes remain localized, reducing ripple effects. UML modeling provides a clear blueprint for identifying potential scalability challenges early in the design process. OOAD principles like low coupling and high cohesion further support distributed architectures and parallel development. By focusing on object-oriented structures, OOAD facilitates horizontal and vertical scalability in modern software systems.

31. What is the difference between generalization and specialization in OOAD?
Answer: Generalization and specialization are complementary concepts in OOAD used to model hierarchical relationships between classes. Generalization involves abstracting common characteristics from multiple subclasses into a single superclass, promoting code reuse and simplifying design. For instance, "Car" and "Truck" can be generalized into a superclass "Vehicle." Specialization, conversely, involves creating subclasses from a general class to define more specific behaviors or attributes. For example, "Vehicle" can be specialized into "Car" and "Truck." While generalization focuses on identifying shared traits, specialization emphasizes extending and refining a base class to meet specific requirements within the system.

32. Explain object diagrams and their use in OOAD.
Answer: Object diagrams in OOAD represent a snapshot of instances (objects) and their relationships at a particular moment in time. Unlike class diagrams, which show general system structure, object diagrams depict actual data values and object states during runtime. They are useful for visualizing examples of object configurations, debugging, and validating system design against requirements. Object diagrams help developers understand how classes interact in real scenarios and are often employed during analysis and testing phases to ensure the design behaves as intended under specific conditions.

33. What is the role of constructors in object-oriented programming?
Answer: Constructors are special methods in object-oriented programming that initialize new objects when they are created. They set initial values for attributes and perform any setup tasks necessary for the object's proper functioning. Constructors have the same name as the class and are automatically invoked upon object instantiation. They can also be overloaded to support multiple ways of initializing an object with different parameter sets. In OOAD, constructors support encapsulation and ensure objects are created in a consistent, predictable state, reducing errors and improving system stability.

34. How does OOAD facilitate code reusability in software projects?
Answer: OOAD facilitates code reusability by organizing software into modular, self-contained objects and classes that can be reused across different parts of a system or even in other projects. Principles like inheritance allow developers to extend existing classes rather than creating new ones from scratch. Encapsulation hides implementation details, enabling developers to reuse objects without worrying about their internal complexities. Polymorphism supports the use of generic interfaces for diverse object types. Design patterns and UML diagrams further guide reusable architecture creation. Code reusability reduces development time, lowers costs, and enhances software reliability and maintainability.

35. What is the difference between aggregation and association in OOAD?
Answer: Association in OOAD represents a general relationship between two classes, where one class knows about or interacts with another. For example, a "Teacher" may be associated with multiple "Students." Aggregation is a specialized form of association that depicts a "whole-part" relationship where the part can exist independently of the whole. For instance, a "Team" aggregates "Players," but players can exist outside the team context. Aggregation is indicated in UML with a hollow diamond, whereas simple association uses a straight line. Aggregation emphasizes a stronger connection than general association but remains weaker than composition.

36. Explain multiple inheritance and its advantages and disadvantages.
Answer: Multiple inheritance allows a class to inherit attributes and methods from more than one superclass. It offers flexibility by enabling a subclass to combine functionalities from multiple sources. For example, a class "FlyingCar" could inherit from both "Car" and "Aircraft" classes. Advantages include improved code reuse and the ability to model complex relationships. However, disadvantages include increased system complexity and ambiguity, such as the "diamond problem," where the compiler must resolve which parent's method to use. Many modern languages like Java avoid multiple inheritance for classes, instead supporting it through interfaces to mitigate these issues.

37. What is the significance of interfaces in OOAD?
Answer: Interfaces in OOAD define a contract of method signatures that implementing classes must fulfill, without providing any implementation details. They support abstraction by specifying what a class should do rather than how it should do it. Interfaces promote flexibility, as multiple unrelated classes can implement the same interface, allowing polymorphic behavior. In Java, for example, an interface "Printable" may require implementing classes to define a print() method. Interfaces are essential in large systems for achieving loose coupling, supporting multiple inheritance-like behavior, and enabling developers to design extensible and testable software architectures.

38. How do sequence diagrams differ from activity diagrams in UML?
Answer: Sequence diagrams and activity diagrams in UML serve different purposes. Sequence diagrams focus on object interactions by showing the sequence of messages exchanged between objects over time to accomplish a specific task. They emphasize time ordering and lifelines. Activity diagrams, on the other hand, represent the flow of activities or processes in a system, highlighting decisions, parallel actions, and workflows without focusing on object interactions. While sequence diagrams are ideal for modeling detailed interactions in use cases, activity diagrams are suited for visualizing overall process logic and business workflows.

39. Explain static polymorphism with an example.
Answer: Static polymorphism, also known as compile-time polymorphism, allows a method or operator to behave differently based on input parameters during compilation. It is achieved through method overloading and operator overloading. For example, in a class "Calculator," there may be two add() methods: one accepting two integers and another accepting two floats. The compiler determines which method to invoke based on the provided arguments. Static polymorphism enhances flexibility and readability but lacks runtime adaptability. Unlike dynamic

polymorphism, static polymorphism is resolved before the program runs, ensuring faster execution in certain scenarios.

40. What is a package diagram in UML, and how is it useful?

Answer: A package diagram in UML shows the organization and dependencies among software packages, which are containers for related classes, interfaces, and sub-packages. It helps developers visualize system modularity and manage complexity by grouping logically related elements. Package diagrams are useful for organizing large systems, planning architecture, and identifying dependencies between modules during design. They also facilitate team collaboration by clarifying how different parts of a system interact. Package diagrams improve maintainability and scalability by promoting a structured approach to managing components in object-oriented software development.

41. Explain the concept of design patterns in OOAD with an example.

Answer: Design patterns in OOAD are reusable solutions to common software design problems. They provide templates for structuring code in a way that is efficient, maintainable, and scalable. An example is the Singleton pattern, which ensures that a class has only one instance and provides a global point of access to it. This pattern is often used in logging or configuration systems. Design patterns promote best practices, reduce development time, and simplify communication among developers by offering a shared vocabulary for solving recurring design challenges in object-oriented systems.

42. What is object persistence, and why is it important?

Answer: Object persistence refers to the ability of objects to outlive the execution of a program by saving their state to a storage medium like a database or file system. It allows applications to store and retrieve object data across sessions. Object persistence is critical in software systems where data continuity is required, such as e-commerce platforms storing customer orders. Techniques for achieving persistence include object-relational mapping (ORM) tools like Hibernate. Persistence ensures that important information remains intact even after the program terminates, enhancing usability and reliability in long-running systems.

43. How does OOAD support large-scale system development?

Answer: OOAD supports large-scale system development by emphasizing modularity, reusability, and abstraction, enabling teams to divide complex systems into manageable components. UML modeling helps visualize relationships and workflows, facilitating better planning and coordination among team members. Principles like low coupling and high cohesion allow different teams to work on separate modules with minimal dependencies. Encapsulation and inheritance promote consistent coding practices, while design patterns address recurring architectural challenges. OOAD's emphasis on clear documentation and scalable architectures ensures that large systems remain maintainable and adaptable as requirements evolve over time.

44. Explain the importance of documentation in OOAD.

Answer: Documentation in OOAD serves as a vital reference for developers, analysts, and stakeholders throughout the software development lifecycle. UML diagrams, class specifications, and use case descriptions provide clear insights into system design, behavior, and interactions. Proper documentation ensures consistency, supports onboarding of new team members, and simplifies maintenance and debugging. It acts as a communication bridge between technical and non-technical stakeholders, aligning expectations and reducing misunderstandings. In dynamic environments, well-maintained documentation helps teams adapt to changes efficiently while preserving the integrity of the system's design.

45. What is object cloning, and how is it implemented in OOAD?

Answer: Object cloning involves creating an exact copy of an existing object, including its attributes and current state. It is implemented through techniques like shallow copying, where only top-level fields are duplicated, and deep copying, which creates independent copies of all referenced objects. In Java, for example, the clone() method can be used for this purpose. Object cloning is useful in scenarios like caching, undo mechanisms, or creating temporary object variants for simulations. Challenges include managing references in deep copies and ensuring that cloned objects maintain consistent behavior in complex systems.

46. How do collaboration diagrams differ from sequence diagrams in UML?
Answer: Collaboration diagrams (also known as communication diagrams) and sequence diagrams both model object interactions but differ in emphasis. Sequence diagrams focus on the chronological sequence of messages exchanged between objects, highlighting the time-ordering of events. Collaboration diagrams emphasize the structural organization of objects and the links through which they communicate, with less focus on timing. Collaboration diagrams are useful for visualizing relationships and responsibilities among objects, while sequence diagrams are better for understanding detailed interaction flows. Both diagrams complement each other in OOAD to provide comprehensive insights into system dynamics.

47. What is the difference between class and object in UML diagrams?
Answer: In UML diagrams, a class represents a blueprint defining the structure and behavior of a group of similar objects, including attributes and methods. It is depicted as a rectangle divided into compartments for name, attributes, and operations. An object, on the other hand, is an instance of a class at runtime, representing a specific entity with concrete values for its attributes. In object diagrams, objects are shown with underlined names and attribute values, providing snapshots of real system states. Classes are abstract, while objects are tangible entities created based on class definitions.

48. Explain the concept of encapsulation and how it supports security in software systems.
Answer: Encapsulation supports security in software systems by restricting direct access to an object's internal data and exposing only controlled interfaces. It uses access modifiers like private, protected, and public to define which components can interact with an object's attributes and methods. This approach prevents unauthorized manipulation of data, ensuring that only valid operations are performed through designated methods. Encapsulation enhances maintainability by allowing internal changes without affecting external modules. By hiding sensitive implementation details, encapsulation reduces vulnerabilities and promotes secure, robust software systems in object-oriented design.

49. What is the purpose of deployment diagrams in OOAD?
Answer: Deployment diagrams in OOAD illustrate the physical deployment of software components on hardware nodes, showing how different system parts are distributed across servers, devices, and networks. They model runtime architectures, including communication paths between nodes and the allocation of components to hardware. Deployment diagrams are essential for understanding system scalability, performance, and security considerations. They help developers and administrators plan infrastructure requirements and ensure that the designed architecture aligns with hardware constraints and operational goals. These diagrams play a crucial role during the deployment and maintenance phases of software systems.

50. How does OOAD enhance system scalability and maintainability?
Answer: OOAD enhances system scalability and maintainability by encouraging modular, reusable, and loosely coupled designs. Encapsulation isolates changes within specific classes, minimizing ripple effects across the system. Inheritance and polymorphism allow developers to extend functionality without modifying existing code, supporting system evolution. UML diagrams provide clear documentation of structure and behavior, aiding maintenance and debugging. OOAD's emphasis on high cohesion ensures each class has a focused responsibility, simplifying updates and reducing complexity. Together, these principles create software systems that can scale to accommodate growth and remain manageable over time.

51. What is object-oriented decomposition, and how does it benefit software design?
Answer: Object-oriented decomposition involves breaking down a system into smaller, manageable components based on objects that represent real-world entities. Each object encapsulates data and behaviors relevant to its role in the system. This approach benefits software design by promoting modularity, making the system easier to develop, test, and maintain. It supports code reuse through inheritance and polymorphism and aligns closely with user requirements by modeling familiar concepts. Object-oriented decomposition also enhances collaboration, as different teams can work on distinct components independently while ensuring seamless integration during system assembly.

52. Explain the difference between static binding and dynamic binding with examples.
Answer: Static binding, or early binding, resolves method calls at compile time. For instance, method overloading in a class uses static binding because the compiler determines which method version to invoke based on parameter types. Dynamic binding, or late binding, occurs at runtime and is used in method overriding, where the actual object type

determines which method is executed. For example, if a base class reference points to a derived class object, the derived class's overridden method is called at runtime. Static binding ensures faster execution, while dynamic binding provides flexibility and supports polymorphism.

53. What is object responsibility in OOAD, and why is it important?
Answer: Object responsibility refers to the set of tasks or functions assigned to an object in a system. It defines what the object knows (attributes) and what it does (methods). Clearly defining responsibilities ensures that objects are cohesive, focusing on a single, well-defined purpose. This practice simplifies system design, promotes reusability, and reduces coupling between components. Assigning appropriate responsibilities supports maintainability and scalability by allowing developers to modify or extend functionality without affecting unrelated parts of the system, making object responsibility a cornerstone of robust object-oriented software design.

54. How does OOAD support iterative and incremental software development?
Answer: OOAD aligns well with iterative and incremental software development methodologies, such as Agile, by allowing systems to evolve through repeated cycles of analysis, design, and implementation. Developers model small, functional parts of the system using UML diagrams, build prototypes, and refine them based on stakeholder feedback. This approach reduces risks by catching design flaws early and supports flexible responses to changing requirements. OOAD's modular nature facilitates incremental integration of new features while maintaining overall system integrity. This compatibility makes OOAD ideal for modern software projects requiring adaptability and continuous improvement.

55. What is the purpose of CRC cards in object-oriented design?
Answer: CRC (Class-Responsibility-Collaborator) cards are a lightweight modeling tool used in object-oriented design to represent classes, their responsibilities, and the other classes they collaborate with. Each card includes the class name, a list of its responsibilities, and the collaborators it interacts with to fulfill those responsibilities. CRC cards encourage brainstorming and promote team discussions during early design phases. They help developers identify appropriate class boundaries, assign clear responsibilities, and design low-coupled, cohesive systems. CRC cards are particularly useful for visualizing high-level designs before transitioning to detailed UML diagrams.

56. Explain the concept of reusability in OOAD with examples.
Answer: Reusability in OOAD refers to designing software components, such as classes and methods, so they can be employed in multiple applications or contexts without modification. For example, a "PaymentProcessor" class can be reused across e-commerce, subscription, and banking systems. Principles like encapsulation, inheritance, and polymorphism promote reusability by isolating functionality and allowing extensions without altering existing code. Design patterns further enhance reusability by providing standardized solutions to common design challenges. Reusability reduces development time, minimizes errors, and lowers costs, making it a key objective in object-oriented software engineering.

57. How does OOAD support better alignment with real-world systems?
Answer: OOAD supports better alignment with real-world systems by modeling software components as objects that represent real-world entities and their interactions. This approach makes designs intuitive for developers and stakeholders alike, as classes and objects reflect tangible concepts like "Customer," "Invoice," or "Order." By focusing on encapsulating attributes and behaviors within objects, OOAD mirrors how entities operate in reality. This alignment improves requirement gathering, enhances communication with non-technical users, and results in systems that are easier to understand, validate, and maintain throughout their lifecycle.

58. What are stereotypes in UML, and how are they used?
Answer: Stereotypes in UML are extensions of standard modeling elements that allow developers to create new types of elements tailored to specific domains or contexts. They add semantic meaning and help differentiate customized elements from standard ones. Stereotypes are enclosed in guillemets (<< >>) and applied to classes, components, or relationships. For example, <<interface>> indicates a class is an interface, while <<controller>> marks a class as part of the control layer in an architecture. Stereotypes improve clarity and provide additional information without altering the core UML syntax, supporting clearer and more expressive designs.

59. Explain the difference between abstract classes and concrete classes in OOAD.

Answer: Abstract classes in OOAD serve as base templates that define common attributes and methods but cannot be instantiated directly. They often include abstract methods without implementations, which must be defined in derived subclasses. Concrete classes, on the other hand, are fully implemented and can create objects. For example, an abstract class "Shape" may define an abstract method draw(), which is implemented differently in concrete subclasses like "Circle" and "Rectangle." Abstract classes promote code reuse and enforce consistency, while concrete classes represent functional, instantiable entities in object-oriented systems.

60. What is the difference between functional decomposition and object-oriented decomposition?

Answer: Functional decomposition breaks down a system into functions or procedures based on tasks or operations, focusing on "what the system does." It is common in procedural programming. Object-oriented decomposition, in contrast, organizes systems around objects representing real-world entities, focusing on "who does what" and encapsulating both data and behavior. OOAD's object-oriented decomposition supports modularity, reusability, and scalability, aligning more naturally with complex, evolving systems. While functional decomposition may lead to tightly coupled code, object-oriented decomposition promotes loosely coupled designs that are easier to maintain and extend.

61. How does OOAD facilitate team collaboration in software projects?

Answer: OOAD facilitates team collaboration by providing clear visual models, like UML diagrams, that represent system structure and behavior. These models serve as a shared reference point for developers, analysts, and stakeholders, reducing misunderstandings and aligning expectations. The modular design in OOAD allows teams to work on separate components independently, promoting parallel development and reducing integration issues. Encapsulation ensures changes in one module have minimal impact on others, supporting collaborative workflows. Additionally, design patterns and standardized documentation in OOAD provide consistent guidelines that help teams coordinate efforts efficiently.

62. Explain the concept of visibility modifiers in OOAD.

Answer: Visibility modifiers in OOAD define the level of access control for class attributes and methods, supporting encapsulation and information hiding. The three main modifiers are public (+), private (-), and protected (#). Public members are accessible from any class, private members are restricted to the defining class, and protected members are accessible within the defining class and its subclasses. Proper use of visibility modifiers ensures that only necessary details are exposed, protecting the integrity of an object's state and reducing the likelihood of unintended interactions between components in an object-oriented system.

63. What is the difference between class-level and instance-level attributes?

Answer: Class-level attributes, also known as static attributes, are shared across all instances of a class and belong to the class itself. They are defined using the static keyword in many programming languages. Instance-level attributes, in contrast, are unique to each object created from the class and store data specific to that object. For example, in a "Car" class, a static attribute might track the total number of cars produced, while instance attributes like color and model vary per car. Understanding this distinction is vital for managing shared and individual data correctly in object-oriented systems.

64. Explain the concept of delegation in object-oriented systems.

Answer: Delegation in object-oriented systems refers to an object handing off a task or responsibility to another object, which performs the operation on its behalf. This design approach promotes code reuse and simplifies class responsibilities by allowing specialized classes to handle specific behaviors. For example, a "Printer" class might delegate formatting tasks to a separate "Formatter" class. Delegation supports flexibility, as behaviors can be changed dynamically by swapping delegate objects. It also aligns with the principle of composition over inheritance, promoting loosely coupled and maintainable software architectures in OOAD.

65. What are the advantages of using UML activity diagrams in software design?

Answer: UML activity diagrams offer several advantages in software design. They visually represent workflows, decision points, and parallel processes, helping developers and stakeholders understand system behavior and logic. Activity diagrams are particularly effective for modeling business processes, use case flows, and complex algorithms. They facilitate early detection of potential bottlenecks or logical errors and support communication across technical and non-technical teams. By providing a clear, high-level view of system activities, these diagrams streamline requirement analysis, enhance collaboration, and guide the development of efficient, well-structured software systems.

66. How does OOAD address software complexity in large systems?
Answer: OOAD addresses software complexity by breaking down large systems into modular, manageable components that mirror real-world entities. Encapsulation hides internal details, simplifying interactions between components. Inheritance and polymorphism promote code reuse and flexibility, while UML diagrams provide clear visual representations of system architecture and behavior. This structured approach helps developers focus on individual parts without being overwhelmed by the entire system. OOAD also supports incremental development, allowing teams to build and integrate components step by step, making large, complex systems easier to design, implement, and maintain.

67. Explain the concept of object identity and state in OOAD.
Answer: In OOAD, object identity refers to the unique property of an object that distinguishes it from other objects, even if they have identical attribute values. Each object has a unique identifier or memory reference. Object state, on the other hand, represents the current values of its attributes, which can change over time. Together, identity and state allow systems to track individual objects and their behaviors throughout their lifecycle. These concepts are crucial for modeling dynamic systems accurately, ensuring consistent behavior and proper management of object interactions.

68. What is the role of object-oriented design principles in system evolution?
Answer: Object-oriented design principles such as encapsulation, inheritance, and polymorphism play a vital role in system evolution by supporting adaptability and scalability. Encapsulation isolates changes within classes, reducing the risk of unintended side effects. Inheritance allows new features to be added through subclasses, while polymorphism enables flexible behavior extensions without altering existing code. Principles like low coupling and high cohesion promote modularity, making systems easier to modify and extend over time. By adhering to these principles, OOAD facilitates the continuous evolution of software systems to meet changing user needs and technological advancements.

69. How does OOAD promote software reuse in enterprise systems?
Answer: OOAD promotes software reuse in enterprise systems by creating modular, well-encapsulated components that can be integrated across multiple applications. Inheritance allows common functionalities to be defined in base classes and reused in specialized subclasses. Polymorphism enables generic code that works with diverse object types. Design patterns standardize reusable solutions for recurring problems, and UML models support clear documentation for integrating components. This focus on reuse reduces development costs, improves consistency across systems, and accelerates the deployment of enterprise solutions by leveraging proven, well-tested modules.

70. Explain the concept of object collaboration in OOAD.
Answer: Object collaboration in OOAD refers to how objects interact and work together to perform system tasks. Each object has defined responsibilities and communicates with other objects by sending and receiving messages. Collaboration diagrams (or communication diagrams) in UML illustrate these interactions, showing how objects are linked and which messages flow between them. Effective object collaboration ensures that responsibilities are well-distributed, promoting high cohesion and low coupling. This approach supports maintainability and scalability, as changes in one object have minimal impact on others, fostering robust and adaptable software architectures.

71. What is the significance of high cohesion in object-oriented systems?
Answer: High cohesion in object-oriented systems refers to the degree to which the responsibilities of a class or module are closely related and focused on a single task. It ensures that each component has a well-defined purpose, making the system easier to understand, maintain, and extend. High cohesion reduces complexity by minimizing interdependencies within the module and promotes reusability because the component performs a specific function effectively. In OOAD, focusing on high cohesion results in cleaner designs where changes in one part of the system have minimal impact on others, thus improving overall software quality.

72. Explain the difference between static and dynamic polymorphism.
Answer: Static polymorphism, also called compile-time polymorphism, is resolved by the compiler and includes

method overloading and operator overloading. It allows multiple methods in the same class to have the same name but differ in parameters. Dynamic polymorphism, or runtime polymorphism, is resolved during program execution and involves method overriding in inheritance hierarchies. For instance, a superclass reference calling an overridden method executes the version defined in the subclass. Static polymorphism offers faster performance, while dynamic polymorphism provides flexibility and supports more adaptable designs in complex object-oriented systems.

73. How does OOAD support abstraction in system design?
Answer: OOAD supports abstraction by enabling designers to focus on essential system features while hiding unnecessary implementation details. Classes and interfaces are used to model real-world entities at an abstract level, defining what a system does rather than how it does it. Abstraction simplifies complexity by creating a conceptual model that is easier for developers and stakeholders to understand. In practice, abstract classes and interfaces define shared behaviors for multiple objects, while specific details are implemented in subclasses. This approach facilitates flexible and extensible system designs that adapt well to changing requirements.

74. What is the role of object relationships in OOAD?
Answer: Object relationships in OOAD define how objects interact and depend on one another within a system. They include associations (e.g., "a teacher teaches students"), aggregations (e.g., "a library has books"), compositions (e.g., "a car is composed of an engine"), and dependencies (e.g., "a printer depends on ink"). Modeling relationships accurately ensures that objects collaborate effectively to fulfill system requirements. UML diagrams such as class diagrams visually represent these relationships. Understanding object relationships helps designers create systems with low coupling and high cohesion, promoting maintainability and scalability.

75. Explain the concept of object-oriented metrics and their significance.
Answer: Object-oriented metrics are quantitative measures used to assess the quality, complexity, and maintainability of object-oriented software systems. Common metrics include coupling between classes (CBO), lack of cohesion in methods (LCOM), and depth of inheritance tree (DIT). These metrics help identify potential design flaws such as excessive coupling or low cohesion. By analyzing these aspects, developers can refactor code to improve readability, maintainability, and performance. Object-oriented metrics provide a scientific approach to evaluating and optimizing designs, ensuring that the system adheres to best practices and can evolve efficiently over time.

76. What is a class-responsibility-collaboration (CRC) model in OOAD?
Answer: The CRC model is a lightweight design tool used in OOAD to identify and define classes, their responsibilities, and their collaborators. Each CRC card represents a class, listing its main functions and the other classes it interacts with to fulfill those functions. The CRC model promotes high cohesion by encouraging designers to assign clear and focused responsibilities to each class. It also supports low coupling by highlighting collaborations. The CRC approach is particularly useful during brainstorming sessions, allowing teams to visualize object roles and relationships before creating detailed UML diagrams.

77. How does OOAD support system extensibility?
Answer: OOAD supports system extensibility through modular, flexible designs that accommodate new features with minimal impact on existing components. Principles like inheritance allow developers to extend functionality by creating subclasses, while polymorphism enables the addition of new object types without altering existing code. Encapsulation ensures that changes remain localized, reducing the risk of unintended side effects. Design patterns like Factory and Observer further promote extensibility by providing standardized ways to adapt systems dynamically. OOAD's emphasis on clear responsibilities and low coupling makes it easier to evolve software as user requirements and technologies change.

78. Explain the concept of design by contract in object-oriented programming.
Answer: Design by contract (DbC) is a methodology in object-oriented programming where software components communicate based on precisely defined agreements. Each method or class defines preconditions (what must be true before execution), postconditions (what will be true after execution), and invariants (conditions that remain unchanged). DbC ensures that responsibilities between objects are clear, preventing misuse and improving system reliability. For example, a method withdrawing money from an account might specify that the balance must be sufficient (precondition) and that the account balance decreases accordingly (postcondition). DbC enhances code quality and simplifies debugging in complex systems.

79. What is the difference between a sequence diagram and a collaboration diagram?
Answer: Both sequence and collaboration diagrams model interactions between objects, but they emphasize different aspects. A sequence diagram highlights the chronological order of messages exchanged between objects, focusing on time sequences along vertical lifelines. It is useful for understanding the timing and flow of operations. A collaboration diagram (also called a communication diagram) emphasizes the structural relationships between objects and shows message flows along object links without focusing on time ordering. Sequence diagrams are better for analyzing detailed interactions, while collaboration diagrams provide a broader view of how objects collaborate structurally.

80. How does encapsulation promote loose coupling in OOAD?
Answer: Encapsulation promotes loose coupling by hiding the internal details of a class and exposing only well-defined interfaces for interaction. This ensures that external components interact with the class only through its public methods, without relying on its internal structure. As a result, changes within the class do not affect other parts of the system, reducing dependencies between modules. Loose coupling improves maintainability, as developers can modify or replace components independently. By enforcing encapsulation, OOAD creates robust systems where components remain isolated yet collaborate effectively through clear and stable interfaces.

81. Explain object-oriented software lifecycle and its phases.
Answer: The object-oriented software lifecycle consists of phases that guide system development using object-oriented principles. It begins with requirements gathering and analysis, where use case models and class diagrams capture user needs. Design involves refining these models into detailed architectures using UML diagrams. Implementation translates designs into object-oriented code. Testing ensures that components function correctly, focusing on unit and integration testing of classes and objects. Deployment delivers the system to users, followed by maintenance, where changes and enhancements are managed. This lifecycle emphasizes iterative development, enabling systems to evolve alongside user requirements.

82. What is the difference between static and dynamic models in UML?
Answer: Static models in UML represent the structural aspects of a system, such as classes, attributes, methods, and their relationships. Examples include class diagrams and object diagrams, which provide a blueprint of system architecture. Dynamic models, on the other hand, depict behavioral aspects, showing how objects interact over time and respond to events. Examples include sequence diagrams, activity diagrams, and state diagrams. Static models answer "what" exists in the system, while dynamic models address "how" components behave and collaborate, offering complementary perspectives in OOAD.

83. How does inheritance reduce code duplication in software systems?
Answer: Inheritance reduces code duplication by allowing common attributes and methods to be defined in a base class and reused across multiple derived classes. For example, a base class "Employee" may include shared properties like name and ID, which subclasses like "Manager" and "Engineer" inherit automatically. This eliminates the need to rewrite the same code in each subclass. Inheritance also promotes maintainability, as changes to shared functionality in the base class propagate to all derived classes. By centralizing common logic, inheritance ensures consistency and reduces errors in object-oriented systems.

84. What is the purpose of activity diagrams in modeling business processes?
Answer: Activity diagrams in UML visually represent workflows, decision points, and parallel processes, making them ideal for modeling business processes. They help stakeholders and developers understand how tasks flow, identify bottlenecks, and ensure that all scenarios are accounted for. In OOAD, activity diagrams bridge the gap between requirements and implementation by clarifying system behavior during different stages of a process. They support the design of use cases, algorithms, and system logic, ensuring that workflows are efficient and align with organizational goals.

85. Explain the concept of object immutability and its advantages.
Answer: Object immutability means that once an object is created, its state cannot be modified. Instead, any changes result in the creation of a new object. Immutable objects are common in functional programming but are also useful in object-oriented systems for ensuring thread safety and predictability. For example, Java's String class is immutable. Advantages include simplified debugging, as object states remain consistent, and protection against unintended side

effects from shared references. Immutability is especially valuable in concurrent systems where multiple threads may access the same objects simultaneously.

86. How does OOAD support software scalability in distributed systems?

Answer: OOAD supports software scalability in distributed systems through modular, loosely coupled designs that facilitate the distribution of components across multiple servers. Encapsulation isolates changes within objects, making it easier to scale individual modules without affecting others. Inheritance and polymorphism allow developers to extend system functionality dynamically. Design patterns like Proxy and Singleton optimize resource usage in distributed environments. UML models help visualize system architecture, enabling better planning for horizontal and vertical scaling. OOAD's focus on reusability and adaptability ensures that systems can handle increasing loads efficiently.

87. What is the difference between strong and weak aggregation in UML?

Answer: Strong aggregation, also known as composition, represents a "whole-part" relationship where the lifetime of the part depends on the whole. For example, if a "House" object is destroyed, its "Room" objects cease to exist. Composition is denoted with a filled diamond in UML. Weak aggregation, or simple aggregation, indicates a looser relationship where the part can exist independently of the whole, such as a "Library" aggregating "Books." It is denoted with a hollow diamond in UML. Understanding these distinctions helps designers model object relationships accurately in OOAD.

88. How does OOAD improve communication between stakeholders?

Answer: OOAD improves communication between stakeholders by using visual models like UML diagrams to represent system structure and behavior in a clear, standardized format. Use case diagrams help stakeholders understand functional requirements, while class and sequence diagrams detail system design for developers. These visual tools bridge the gap between technical and non-technical audiences, ensuring alignment on system goals and expectations. OOAD also promotes iterative development, allowing stakeholders to provide feedback early and often, reducing misunderstandings and ensuring that the final product meets user needs effectively.

89. What is the role of object state in dynamic modeling?

Answer: Object state in dynamic modeling represents the condition of an object at a specific moment, determined by the values of its attributes. State changes occur in response to events or method calls. Dynamic models, such as state diagrams, capture these changes and show how an object transitions between states during its lifecycle. Understanding object states is crucial for designing systems where behavior depends on historical actions, such as order processing systems. Modeling object states ensures predictable and correct responses to different inputs, enhancing system reliability.

90. Explain the concept of object-oriented testing and its strategies.

Answer: Object-oriented testing focuses on verifying the correctness of object-oriented software by testing classes, objects, and their interactions. Strategies include unit testing individual classes and methods, integration testing object collaborations, and system testing overall functionality. Techniques like state-based testing validate object behavior in different states, while inheritance-based testing ensures that subclasses maintain the integrity of parent class contracts. Tools like JUnit facilitate automated testing. Object-oriented testing ensures robust, error-free systems by addressing the unique challenges posed by encapsulation, polymorphism, and inheritance in OOAD designs.

91. What is the significance of object behavior in OOAD?

Answer: Object behavior in OOAD refers to the actions an object can perform in response to messages or method calls. It defines how objects interact with each other and change their state to fulfill system requirements. Modeling behavior is essential because it determines how the system responds to different scenarios. Behavioral diagrams like sequence and state diagrams in UML help designers visualize and analyze object interactions. Understanding object behavior ensures consistency, reduces errors, and allows developers to create predictable and adaptable systems that closely align with real-world processes and user expectations.

92. Explain the concept of method overriding in object-oriented programming.

Answer: Method overriding allows a subclass to provide a specific implementation for a method already defined in its superclass. The overridden method in the subclass must have the same name, parameters, and return type as the one in the parent class. When a superclass reference points to a subclass object, the subclass's method is invoked at runtime, enabling dynamic polymorphism. This feature supports extensibility and flexibility in object-oriented systems by allowing subclasses to customize inherited behavior while maintaining a consistent interface for interacting with different object types.

93. How does OOAD promote system adaptability to changing requirements?
Answer: OOAD promotes system adaptability by emphasizing modularity, encapsulation, and flexible design principles. Objects are designed to encapsulate their data and behaviors, enabling localized changes without affecting other parts of the system. Inheritance allows new features to be added through subclasses, while polymorphism enables dynamic behavior adjustments at runtime. UML modeling provides clear blueprints for analyzing potential impacts of changes. Design patterns like Strategy and Observer also support adaptability by decoupling system components. This approach ensures that software can evolve efficiently in response to changing user requirements or technological advancements.

94. What is the role of object collaboration in use case realization?
Answer: In use case realization, object collaboration defines how multiple objects interact to achieve the behavior described in a use case. Each object plays a specific role, sending and receiving messages to fulfill its responsibilities. Collaboration diagrams and sequence diagrams in UML help visualize these interactions, showing the flow of control and data among objects. Understanding object collaboration ensures that system functionality is distributed logically across components, supporting modularity and reuse. It also helps identify potential bottlenecks or design flaws early in the development process.

95. Explain the purpose of object roles in OOAD.
Answer: Object roles in OOAD describe the specific function or responsibility an object assumes within a particular context or scenario. A single object may have different roles in different collaborations, allowing it to participate flexibly in various system behaviors. For example, a "User" object may act as an "Customer" in one process and as an "Administrator" in another. Defining clear roles ensures proper distribution of responsibilities, supports reusable designs, and facilitates better understanding of object interactions during system analysis and modeling.

96. How does OOAD handle real-time system requirements?
Answer: OOAD addresses real-time system requirements by modeling objects that represent both hardware and software components, encapsulating their behaviors and interactions. UML diagrams like state and sequence diagrams help analyze timing constraints, event handling, and concurrency. Real-time design patterns, such as Reactor and Scheduler, support predictable and efficient response times. Encapsulation and modularity enable developers to manage complexity and isolate time-critical components. OOAD's iterative approach allows real-time systems to be tested and refined incrementally, ensuring they meet strict performance and reliability requirements.

97. What is the importance of inheritance hierarchies in OOAD?
Answer: Inheritance hierarchies organize classes into parent-child relationships, allowing shared attributes and methods to be defined in base classes and reused in derived classes. This structure simplifies system design by promoting code reuse and reducing redundancy. Inheritance hierarchies also support polymorphism, enabling flexible behavior across different object types. However, careful design is required to avoid deep or overly complex hierarchies, which can make systems harder to maintain. Well-structured inheritance hierarchies improve maintainability, extensibility, and consistency in object-oriented software systems.

98. Explain the difference between object association and dependency in UML.
Answer: Object association in UML represents a structural relationship where one object is linked to another, often indicating that they interact or share information. For example, a "Teacher" and "Student" may be associated in a school management system. Dependency, on the other hand, is a weaker relationship indicating that a change in one class may affect another, but there is no persistent connection. For example, a "ReportGenerator" class may depend on a "Printer" class to produce output. Understanding these differences helps model accurate relationships and interactions in OOAD.

99. How does OOAD support user-centric system design?
Answer: OOAD supports user-centric system design by focusing on modeling real-world entities and their interactions in ways that align with user expectations. Use case diagrams capture user requirements and system behavior from the perspective of external actors, ensuring the software meets functional needs. Objects are designed to represent familiar concepts, simplifying understanding and validation. Iterative development cycles in OOAD involve frequent stakeholder feedback, allowing refinements based on user input. This approach results in systems that are intuitive, user-friendly, and capable of addressing real-world challenges effectively.

100. What is the purpose of object-oriented frameworks in software development?
Answer: Object-oriented frameworks provide reusable, pre-defined structures and components that developers can extend and customize for specific applications. They define common patterns and best practices, accelerating development by handling repetitive tasks such as user interface management or database access. Examples include Java's Spring Framework and .NET Framework. Frameworks promote consistency, reduce errors, and support maintainability by encouraging modular and well-organized designs. In OOAD, frameworks serve as foundational building blocks that allow teams to focus on business logic rather than low-level infrastructure concerns.

101. Explain the difference between shallow and deep copy in OOAD.
Answer: A shallow copy duplicates an object's top-level structure but shares references to nested objects, meaning changes to nested objects affect both copies. In contrast, a deep copy creates entirely independent duplicates of the object and all nested objects, ensuring complete isolation between the original and the copy. For example, copying a "Document" object with a shallow copy would duplicate the main object but share references to embedded images, whereas a deep copy would also duplicate the images. Deep copies are more resource-intensive but necessary in systems requiring independent object states.

102. How does OOAD improve system traceability?
Answer: OOAD improves system traceability by providing clear mappings between requirements, design components, and implementation artifacts. UML diagrams like use case diagrams connect functional requirements to system behaviors, while class diagrams and sequence diagrams map these behaviors to specific objects and interactions. This traceability simplifies impact analysis when changes occur and ensures that all user needs are addressed during development. It also supports testing and validation by allowing teams to trace test cases back to original requirements, ensuring system correctness and completeness.

103. What is the importance of object hierarchies in software architecture?
Answer: Object hierarchies organize classes and objects in structured levels, allowing shared functionality to be abstracted in higher levels and specialized behavior to be implemented in lower levels. This promotes code reuse, reduces redundancy, and supports polymorphism by enabling generic interactions with objects at higher levels. In software architecture, well-designed hierarchies simplify system organization, enhance maintainability, and provide a clear roadmap for developers. They also support scalability by allowing new object types to be added without disrupting existing structures.

104. Explain the concept of object-oriented refactoring.
Answer: Object-oriented refactoring involves restructuring existing code to improve its internal design without changing external behavior. Common refactoring techniques include renaming classes for clarity, extracting methods to simplify complex code, and applying design patterns like Strategy or Observer. Refactoring enhances readability, maintainability, and performance while preserving functionality. In OOAD, refactoring is often guided by principles like low coupling and high cohesion, ensuring that system improvements align with best practices. Regular refactoring prevents code decay and supports the long-term evolution of software systems.

105. How does OOAD support parallel development in software teams?
Answer: OOAD supports parallel development by dividing systems into modular, loosely coupled components represented by classes and objects. UML diagrams provide clear documentation of interfaces and interactions, enabling teams to work independently on different parts of the system without conflicts. Encapsulation ensures that changes within one module do not affect others, reducing integration issues. Design patterns like Facade further facilitate modular development by defining clear entry points for subsystems. This approach allows large teams to collaborate effectively, accelerating development and improving productivity.

106. What is object pooling, and why is it used in OOAD?
Answer: Object pooling is a design pattern where a set of pre-instantiated objects is maintained in a pool for reuse, rather than creating and destroying objects repeatedly. This approach improves performance by reducing the overhead associated with object creation and garbage collection, especially in systems requiring frequent object instantiation, like database connections or thread management. In OOAD, object pooling supports resource optimization and scalability, making it valuable for high-performance and real-time systems.

107. Explain the concept of persistence in OOAD with examples.
Answer: Persistence in OOAD refers to the ability of objects to retain their state across program executions by storing data in a permanent medium like a database or file system. For example, a "Customer" object's details can be saved to a database and reloaded later when needed. Object-relational mapping (ORM) frameworks like Hibernate facilitate persistence by mapping object attributes to relational tables. Persistence ensures data continuity and is critical in systems where information must survive application restarts, such as e-commerce platforms or banking systems.

108. How does OOAD promote system robustness?
Answer: OOAD promotes system robustness by designing modular, encapsulated components that can handle errors and adapt to changes gracefully. Encapsulation isolates faults, reducing their impact on other parts of the system. Polymorphism and inheritance allow flexible behavior adjustments, while design patterns like Command and Adapter simplify error recovery. UML modeling helps identify potential failure points and design appropriate safeguards. Together, these practices result in resilient systems that maintain stability and functionality even in unpredictable or adverse conditions.

109. What is the role of object-oriented middleware in distributed systems?
Answer: Object-oriented middleware acts as an intermediary layer that enables communication and data exchange between distributed objects in a networked system. It abstracts the complexities of underlying hardware and network protocols, providing services like object invocation, transaction management, and security. Examples include CORBA and Java RMI. Middleware supports scalability, interoperability, and modularity in distributed object-oriented systems, allowing developers to focus on business logic instead of low-level infrastructure concerns.

110. Explain the difference between association and composition in OOAD.
Answer: Association in OOAD represents a general relationship between two objects, where they can interact but do not depend on each other for existence. For instance, a "Teacher" and "Student" are associated because they interact, but each can exist independently. Composition, on the other hand, is a stronger relationship where one object owns another, and the child object's lifecycle depends on the parent. For example, a "Car" is composed of "Engine" and "Wheels," which cease to exist if the car is destroyed. Composition ensures tighter coupling and clearer ownership in system design.

111. What is object serialization in OOAD, and why is it used?
Answer: Object serialization is the process of converting an object's state into a byte stream so it can be stored in a file, sent over a network, or persisted in a database. Later, the object can be reconstructed using deserialization. Serialization is crucial for transmitting objects between systems in distributed applications or saving the state of an object for future use. In Java, for instance, implementing the `Serializable` interface enables serialization. This process supports data persistence, simplifies object transfer, and is widely used in applications such as caching, session management, and remote method invocation (RMI).

112. Explain the concept of design patterns with an example of the Observer pattern.
Answer: Design patterns are reusable solutions to recurring problems in software design. They provide standardized approaches to structuring code for maintainability and scalability. The Observer pattern is used when an object (subject) needs to notify multiple dependent objects (observers) about changes in its state. For example, in a stock trading application, when the stock price changes, all registered observers (like dashboards or analytics modules) are automatically updated. This pattern promotes loose coupling between the subject and observers, allowing dynamic addition or removal of dependencies at runtime.

113. What is the role of object identity in OOAD?
Answer: Object identity in OOAD distinguishes one object from another, even if they have identical attribute values. Each object possesses a unique identity, often represented by a memory address or an assigned identifier. This concept allows systems to track and manage individual objects independently, maintaining state and relationships accurately. For example, two "Customer" objects with the same name and details are treated as distinct if they have different identities. Object identity is vital in persistence, object referencing, and ensuring data integrity in complex software systems.

114. How does encapsulation contribute to software security in OOAD?
Answer: Encapsulation contributes to software security by hiding the internal state and implementation details of objects, exposing only necessary interfaces to external components. By restricting direct access to sensitive data and requiring interactions through controlled methods, encapsulation prevents unauthorized or unintended modifications. Access modifiers like `private` and `protected` enforce boundaries within a system. This ensures that even if external components misuse the system, critical parts remain secure. Encapsulation also simplifies debugging and supports robust error handling by centralizing validation and protection within well-defined classes.

115. Explain object persistence and how it is implemented in OOAD.
Answer: Object persistence refers to maintaining the state of an object beyond the lifetime of the program that created it. It is implemented by saving object data in external storage, such as databases or files, and restoring it later. In OOAD, persistence frameworks like Hibernate map object-oriented data to relational databases using Object-Relational Mapping (ORM). This allows developers to interact with persistent data as if they were standard objects in the application. Object persistence is crucial in systems like e-commerce platforms, where user and transaction data must remain intact across sessions.

116. What is the difference between composition and inheritance in OOAD?
Answer: Composition and inheritance are two ways to model relationships in OOAD. Inheritance represents an "is-a" relationship, where a subclass inherits attributes and behaviors from a parent class. For example, a "Car" class can inherit from a "Vehicle" class. Composition represents a "has-a" relationship, where one class contains objects of another class as part of its structure, such as a "Car" composed of "Engine" and "Wheel" objects. Composition is favored for flexibility and reducing tight coupling, while inheritance is used when shared functionality needs to be extended across related classes.

117. How does polymorphism improve code flexibility in OOAD?
Answer: Polymorphism allows objects of different classes to be treated as instances of a common superclass, enabling a single interface to represent multiple types. This improves code flexibility by allowing developers to write generic code that works with diverse object types. For example, a method accepting a "Shape" object can handle "Circle" and "Rectangle" objects seamlessly. At runtime, the appropriate method implementation is chosen dynamically. Polymorphism supports extensibility and simplifies system updates, as new object types can be integrated without modifying existing code that depends on the shared interface.

118. What is the significance of UML component diagrams in software design?
Answer: UML component diagrams model the physical structure of a software system by illustrating how software components (e.g., modules, libraries) are organized and interact. They show dependencies between components and the services each provides or requires. Component diagrams are especially useful during the design and deployment phases, helping teams visualize how different parts of a system fit together. They support modular development, enabling teams to work on separate components independently, and assist in planning for system scalability, deployment, and integration.

119. Explain the role of interfaces in promoting loose coupling in OOAD.
Answer: Interfaces promote loose coupling by defining contracts that classes agree to implement without specifying how. This allows classes to interact through shared interfaces rather than depending on concrete implementations. For example, a payment system might define a "PaymentProcessor" interface implemented by multiple classes like "CreditCardProcessor" and "PayPalProcessor." Clients use the interface without knowing the specifics of each

processor. This approach enables developers to swap or extend implementations without altering dependent code, fostering flexibility and maintainability in object-oriented systems.

120. How does OOAD handle concurrency in software systems?

Answer: OOAD handles concurrency by modeling objects that operate independently and interact through message passing or shared resources. Concurrency issues like race conditions and deadlocks are analyzed using UML activity diagrams and sequence diagrams. Patterns such as Monitor, Active Object, and Producer-Consumer support safe concurrent designs. Encapsulation ensures that shared resources are accessed in a controlled manner, often through synchronized methods or locks. OOAD's modular approach allows developers to isolate and test concurrent components, ensuring system stability and predictable behavior under parallel execution.

121. What is the purpose of UML deployment diagrams in OOAD?

Answer: UML deployment diagrams depict the physical deployment of software components on hardware nodes in a system. They illustrate the relationships between software artifacts, such as executables and libraries, and the hardware infrastructure, including servers and devices. Deployment diagrams are critical for understanding system architecture in distributed environments, planning resource allocation, and ensuring performance and scalability requirements are met. They also assist in visualizing communication paths between nodes and identifying potential bottlenecks or vulnerabilities in the system setup.

122. How does OOAD support maintainability in complex software systems?

Answer: OOAD supports maintainability by promoting modular, reusable, and loosely coupled components. Encapsulation isolates changes within specific classes, reducing the impact on other parts of the system. Inheritance and polymorphism allow developers to extend or modify functionality without altering existing code. UML diagrams provide clear documentation of system structure and behavior, making it easier to understand, debug, and update software. OOAD's emphasis on high cohesion ensures that each class focuses on a single responsibility, simplifying testing and modification. These practices collectively ensure long-term maintainability of complex systems.

123. What is the role of abstract classes in OOAD?

Answer: Abstract classes in OOAD serve as blueprints for other classes, providing shared attributes and methods while leaving specific implementations to subclasses. They may contain abstract methods without implementations, enforcing that derived classes provide their own versions. Abstract classes promote code reuse by encapsulating common functionality and ensuring consistency across related classes. For example, an abstract class "Animal" might define a method makeSound(), which subclasses like "Dog" and "Cat" implement differently. Abstract classes support extensibility and maintainability in object-oriented systems.

124. Explain the difference between dependency injection and service locator patterns in OOAD.

Answer: Dependency injection and service locator are two patterns for managing dependencies in OOAD. Dependency injection provides required dependencies directly to a class, often through constructors or setters, promoting explicit and testable designs. Service locator, in contrast, allows classes to retrieve dependencies from a centralized registry, which hides dependency management details. While dependency injection encourages loose coupling and clearer dependencies, service locator provides flexibility but can obscure the system's architecture. Both patterns are useful for managing complex object interactions in modular, scalable software systems.

125. How does OOAD contribute to building scalable and robust enterprise applications?

Answer: OOAD contributes to building scalable and robust enterprise applications by emphasizing modularity, reusability, and abstraction. Encapsulation isolates changes within components, supporting independent development and updates. Inheritance and polymorphism enable flexible behavior extensions without disrupting existing functionality. Design patterns like Singleton and Factory streamline architecture for large systems. UML diagrams provide a clear blueprint for visualizing and optimizing system components. OOAD also promotes loose coupling, ensuring components can scale horizontally or vertically as needed. These practices result in enterprise applications that can handle growth, complexity, and evolving requirements effectively.

Chapter 7: Most Asked Questions Part-B

1. Analyze how the concept of polymorphism simplifies code in a payroll management system.
Answer: In a payroll management system, polymorphism allows different types of employees, such as full-time, part-time, and contract workers, to be treated uniformly through a common interface or base class. For instance, a base class `Employee` might define a method calculateSalary(). Each employee type can provide its own implementation of this method while maintaining a consistent interface for processing payroll. The system can process a list of employees without knowing their specific types, calling calculateSalary() polymorphically. This approach reduces code duplication, simplifies logic, and allows new employee types to be added without modifying existing payroll processing code.

2. Discuss how UML diagrams improve communication between software development teams and stakeholders.
Answer: UML diagrams serve as a visual language that bridges the gap between technical and non-technical stakeholders. They simplify complex system concepts by modeling structure (e.g., class diagrams) and behavior (e.g., sequence diagrams) in a clear, standardized way. Developers use UML to plan and document system design, while stakeholders rely on it to validate requirements. For example, use case diagrams help clarify functional needs, and activity diagrams visualize workflows. This shared understanding reduces miscommunication, aligns expectations, and facilitates collaboration throughout the development lifecycle, leading to software that better meets business objectives.

3. Evaluate the role of encapsulation in managing changes in a large-scale banking application.
Answer: Encapsulation in a large-scale banking application ensures that changes within one module do not impact unrelated parts of the system. By hiding internal implementation details and exposing only necessary interfaces, encapsulation isolates functionalities like account management, loan processing, and transaction validation. If the logic for calculating interest rates changes, only the encapsulated class responsible for this operation needs to be updated. Other components interacting with this class remain unaffected. This modular approach reduces system complexity, improves maintainability, and minimizes the risk of introducing errors during system enhancements.

4. Explain how the Singleton pattern can be used to manage configuration settings in a distributed system.
Answer: The Singleton pattern ensures that only one instance of a configuration settings object exists throughout a distributed system. This centralized instance provides consistent access to settings like database connections, API keys, and application parameters. Using Singleton prevents the creation of multiple configuration objects that might lead to inconsistencies. In a distributed system, a Singleton implementation might be combined with thread-safety techniques or lazy initialization to manage resource access efficiently. This pattern simplifies configuration management and ensures uniform behavior across different components and services in the system.

5. Analyze the advantages of using aggregation in modeling an online shopping system.
Answer: Aggregation in an online shopping system models "has-a" relationships where components can exist independently. For example, a `ShoppingCart` aggregates `Product` objects. Even if the cart is deleted, the products remain in the inventory. This weak relationship reflects real-world scenarios and promotes reusability of classes across multiple contexts. Aggregation allows developers to design flexible systems where objects can interact without tight coupling, supporting features like wishlist management or product recommendation systems. This design enhances modularity and simplifies updates, as changes to one component do not necessitate modifications to others.

6. Assess how object-oriented principles improve software maintainability in healthcare systems.
Answer: Object-oriented principles like encapsulation, inheritance, and polymorphism significantly enhance software maintainability in healthcare systems. Encapsulation isolates critical modules such as patient records and billing, making changes localized and safer. Inheritance supports reusing common functionalities like authentication across different user types (e.g., doctors, nurses, administrators). Polymorphism allows systems to extend support for new medical devices or workflows without modifying existing code. These principles create modular, loosely coupled systems that can evolve as healthcare regulations change, ensuring that software remains compliant and adaptable over time.

7. Examine how activity diagrams can model complex workflows in logistics management systems.
Answer: Activity diagrams provide a clear and visual representation of workflows in logistics management systems, including order processing, shipment tracking, and inventory management. They model decision points, parallel processes, and event-driven actions, enabling stakeholders to understand system logic. For example, an activity diagram can depict the flow of goods from warehouse to delivery, showing how different departments interact. This modeling helps identify bottlenecks, inefficiencies, and potential improvements. Activity diagrams are valuable during analysis and design phases, ensuring that workflows align with operational goals and customer expectations.

8. Describe how object-oriented decomposition supports team-based development in enterprise software projects.
Answer: Object-oriented decomposition breaks down enterprise software into modular, self-contained components like classes and objects, each handling a specific responsibility. This modularity enables teams to work on different system parts—such as user authentication, payment gateways, or reporting—independently. Encapsulation ensures that changes within one module do not disrupt others, reducing integration risks. UML diagrams further guide coordination by clearly documenting interfaces and dependencies. Object-oriented decomposition improves collaboration, accelerates development, and supports parallel workflows, making it ideal for large, distributed teams in enterprise projects.

9. Evaluate the impact of inheritance on code extensibility in object-oriented systems.
Answer: Inheritance promotes code extensibility by allowing developers to create subclasses that inherit and extend functionality from existing classes. This enables the addition of new features without altering base class code, preserving system stability. For example, a `Vehicle` class can serve as the foundation for `Car`, `Bike`, and `Truck` subclasses, each adding specific attributes and behaviors. However, over-reliance on deep inheritance hierarchies can lead to rigid designs. Using composition alongside inheritance can balance extensibility and flexibility, ensuring object-oriented systems remain adaptable and maintainable.

10. Analyze how polymorphism supports runtime flexibility in e-commerce applications.
Answer: Polymorphism allows e-commerce applications to handle different product types, payment methods, or delivery options through common interfaces. For example, a `PaymentProcessor` interface can define a method processPayment(), with implementations for credit cards, PayPal, and digital wallets. At runtime, the appropriate processor is invoked based on user selection. This design supports dynamic behavior and simplifies the integration of new features, such as adding cryptocurrency payments. Polymorphism enables e-commerce systems to adapt to changing customer preferences and business needs without extensive code modifications.

11. Explain how design patterns improve system architecture in object-oriented projects.
Answer: Design patterns offer proven solutions to common architectural challenges, promoting best practices and reducing development effort. Patterns like Factory simplify object creation, Singleton ensures a single point of access to shared resources, and Observer facilitates communication between components. By standardizing design approaches, patterns improve system organization, scalability, and maintainability. They also enhance collaboration among developers by providing a shared vocabulary for complex concepts. In object-oriented projects, applying design patterns leads to robust, modular architectures that are easier to extend and adapt to evolving requirements.

12. Discuss the advantages of using state diagrams to model object behavior.
Answer: State diagrams visualize the lifecycle of objects by illustrating the possible states they can occupy and transitions triggered by events. They are particularly useful for modeling systems where objects exhibit complex behaviors, such as an `Order` object transitioning from “Pending” to “Shipped” to “Delivered.” State diagrams help identify invalid states, clarify workflows, and ensure that all scenarios are handled. In OOAD, they improve system reliability by enabling developers to design predictable and error-free object behaviors, particularly in event-driven or real-time systems.

13. Assess how encapsulation helps in securing user data in financial software.
Answer: Encapsulation secures user data in financial software by restricting direct access to sensitive attributes like account balances and transaction histories. Access is controlled through well-defined methods that validate and sanitize inputs before processing. This prevents unauthorized modifications and protects against common security

vulnerabilities such as data leaks or injection attacks. Encapsulation also facilitates encryption and secure storage practices within classes, ensuring compliance with financial regulations. By isolating critical logic, encapsulation strengthens the overall security posture of financial systems.

14. Evaluate the benefits and drawbacks of using abstract classes in system design.
Answer: Abstract classes provide a template for related classes by defining shared attributes and methods while allowing specific implementations in subclasses. Benefits include code reuse, consistency across subclasses, and the ability to enforce a common interface. For example, an abstract class `Employee` might define methods like calculateSalary() that are implemented differently in subclasses. However, abstract classes support only single inheritance, which can limit flexibility in certain scenarios. Overuse of abstract classes may also lead to rigid hierarchies. Balancing abstract classes with interfaces and composition offers a more adaptable design strategy.

15. Analyze how UML sequence diagrams aid in debugging complex systems.
Answer: UML sequence diagrams depict the flow of messages between objects over time, providing insights into system behavior during execution. They help developers trace the sequence of operations leading to a particular outcome, making it easier to identify logic errors, incorrect message ordering, or unintended interactions. Sequence diagrams also facilitate communication between developers by providing a shared reference for understanding object collaborations. In complex systems with multiple interacting components, these diagrams are invaluable for diagnosing and resolving issues efficiently.

16. Discuss how object pooling enhances performance in high-load systems.
Answer: Object pooling improves performance in high-load systems by reusing pre-instantiated objects rather than creating and destroying them repeatedly. This approach reduces the overhead of memory allocation and garbage collection, particularly for resource-intensive objects like database connections or network sockets. In web servers or gaming applications, object pooling ensures efficient resource management and faster response times. Properly implemented object pooling minimizes latency and supports scalability, but developers must carefully manage object lifecycles to avoid issues like stale or improperly reset objects.

17. Evaluate the use of dependency injection in reducing coupling between components.
Answer: Dependency injection (DI) reduces coupling by externalizing the creation and management of dependencies, allowing components to focus on their core responsibilities. Instead of a class instantiating its dependencies, DI frameworks provide them at runtime. This promotes flexibility, as components can be easily replaced or mocked for testing. In OOAD, DI supports modular design and adheres to the Dependency Inversion Principle. However, overuse of DI frameworks can increase complexity, so it is essential to balance DI with simplicity in system architecture.

18. Explain how object-oriented principles improve testability in software systems.
Answer: Object-oriented principles improve testability by creating modular, loosely coupled systems where components can be tested independently. Encapsulation allows developers to isolate and validate individual classes. Inheritance and polymorphism support the use of mock objects and stubs for testing, enabling the simulation of complex behaviors. Design patterns like Strategy and Observer further enhance testability by decoupling components and enabling targeted unit tests. OOAD's focus on clear interfaces and modularity ensures that tests are easier to design, execute, and maintain throughout the software lifecycle.

19. Analyze the impact of loose coupling on system scalability.
Answer: Loose coupling enables system scalability by minimizing dependencies between components, allowing them to evolve and scale independently. In a microservices architecture, for example, loosely coupled services can be deployed and scaled based on demand without impacting other services. This flexibility supports horizontal scaling, fault isolation, and faster development cycles. In OOAD, loose coupling is achieved through interfaces, dependency injection, and encapsulation, resulting in systems that are more resilient, adaptable, and easier to manage as they grow in size and complexity.

20. Evaluate the use of composition over inheritance in designing flexible systems.
Answer: Favoring composition over inheritance allows systems to achieve flexibility by combining behaviors dynamically rather than relying on rigid hierarchies. Composition involves assembling objects with specific

functionalities, promoting reuse and reducing code duplication. For example, a `Car` object may compose an `Engine` object rather than inheriting from it. This design supports changes in behavior at runtime and avoids issues like the fragility of deep inheritance chains. While inheritance is useful for modeling "is-a" relationships, composition is often better for "has-a" relationships and systems requiring high adaptability.

21. Discuss how object-oriented design supports cloud-native application development.
Answer: Object-oriented design supports cloud-native applications by promoting modular, reusable components that align with containerization and microservices. Encapsulation isolates logic within services, enabling independent deployment and scaling. Inheritance and polymorphism simplify the integration of new functionalities without disrupting existing services. Design patterns like Singleton manage shared resources efficiently in distributed environments. OOAD's emphasis on clear interfaces ensures that services communicate effectively through APIs. This approach facilitates rapid development, scalability, and maintainability in dynamic, cloud-based ecosystems.

22. Assess the role of UML deployment diagrams in planning scalable infrastructures.
Answer: UML deployment diagrams visualize how software components are distributed across physical hardware and network nodes. They assist architects in planning scalable infrastructures by modeling communication paths, resource allocations, and hardware dependencies. Deployment diagrams help identify potential bottlenecks, single points of failure, and security vulnerabilities early in the design phase. In cloud-based systems, they support decisions about load balancing, redundancy, and resource scaling. By providing a clear overview of system architecture, deployment diagrams enable efficient and reliable deployment strategies for large-scale applications.

23. Explain how object-oriented middleware simplifies distributed application development.
Answer: Object-oriented middleware abstracts the complexities of communication and coordination between distributed objects in networked systems. It provides services such as object location transparency, message passing, and transaction management. Technologies like CORBA or Java RMI allow developers to focus on business logic rather than low-level networking details. Middleware supports scalability, fault tolerance, and interoperability in distributed environments, enabling developers to build robust, modular applications that seamlessly span multiple servers and platforms.

24. Evaluate the importance of object hierarchies in modeling organizational structures.
Answer: Object hierarchies effectively model organizational structures by representing general roles in base classes and specific roles in subclasses. For example, an `Employee` class may serve as a parent for `Manager`, `Engineer`, and `Intern` subclasses, each with unique attributes and behaviors. This hierarchy reflects real-world reporting lines and responsibilities, facilitating clear system organization. Properly designed hierarchies promote code reuse, consistency, and extensibility. However, deep hierarchies can become rigid and hard to maintain, so balancing inheritance with composition is crucial for flexible system design.

25. Discuss how OOAD principles contribute to the success of agile software development.
Answer: OOAD principles align closely with agile methodologies by promoting modularity, flexibility, and iterative design. Encapsulation supports localized changes, enabling rapid adaptation to evolving requirements. Inheritance and polymorphism allow systems to extend functionality incrementally without breaking existing code. UML modeling provides lightweight documentation that facilitates team communication and stakeholder engagement. By focusing on small, reusable components, OOAD supports agile practices like continuous integration and delivery, resulting in faster development cycles and higher-quality software.

26. Evaluate the role of use case diagrams in capturing user requirements for complex systems.
Answer: Use case diagrams play a vital role in capturing and visualizing user requirements in complex systems. They provide a high-level view of the system by illustrating interactions between external actors and system functionalities. This approach allows stakeholders to understand what the system is expected to do without focusing on technical details. Use case diagrams simplify requirement gathering by clarifying user expectations and identifying system boundaries. For developers, they serve as a blueprint for implementing core functionalities and for prioritizing features during the design phase. This visualization helps prevent miscommunication and ensures alignment with user needs.

27. Discuss how object-oriented analysis helps identify reusable components in software design.
Answer: Object-oriented analysis focuses on identifying real-world entities and their relationships, enabling developers to model reusable components effectively. By analyzing system requirements and breaking them into classes and objects with well-defined responsibilities, designers can create modular components such as authentication handlers, payment processors, or logging utilities. These components can be reused in different parts of the same application or even in other projects. This approach reduces development time, promotes consistency, and ensures that systems remain maintainable and adaptable as requirements evolve.

28. Analyze the benefits of applying the Factory Method design pattern in software systems.
Answer: The Factory Method pattern provides an interface for creating objects but allows subclasses to decide which class to instantiate. This promotes loose coupling by delegating object creation to specific factories, making systems more flexible and easier to maintain. For example, in a graphics application, a factory can create different shapes like circles or squares based on user input without changing the core logic. This design pattern simplifies adding new object types and supports scalability by adhering to the Open/Closed Principle, allowing systems to grow without modifying existing code.

29. Explain how object-oriented principles support microservices architecture.
Answer: Object-oriented principles align well with microservices architecture by promoting modularity, encapsulation, and loose coupling. Each microservice can be viewed as an independent object with encapsulated data and behavior, interacting with others through APIs. Polymorphism supports flexible service implementations, while inheritance allows common functionalities to be abstracted into base components. This approach enables teams to build, deploy, and scale services independently, fostering agility in development and reducing system complexity. OOAD ensures microservices remain cohesive and maintainable, supporting dynamic business requirements and continuous delivery practices.

30. Assess the use of state diagrams in modeling real-time systems.
Answer: State diagrams are highly effective for modeling real-time systems where objects undergo frequent and complex state transitions. They depict all possible states of an object and the events triggering transitions, helping designers analyze system behavior under different scenarios. In systems like air traffic control or medical devices, state diagrams ensure that each component responds predictably to events, preventing invalid or unsafe states. They also assist in validating requirements and guiding implementation, making real-time systems more robust, reliable, and easier to test.

31. Discuss how polymorphism simplifies code maintenance in large-scale applications.
Answer: Polymorphism simplifies code maintenance by allowing developers to write generic code that works with objects of multiple types through a common interface. In large-scale applications, this means a single method can process various object types without requiring explicit conditional logic for each case. For example, a `draw()` method can work for `Circle`, `Rectangle`, and `Triangle` objects, invoking the correct implementation at runtime. This reduces code duplication, enhances readability, and makes it easier to add new types without modifying existing functionality, thus streamlining maintenance and reducing potential errors.

32. Analyze the advantages of using abstract classes in enterprise software development.
Answer: Abstract classes provide a structured way to define shared attributes and behaviors while allowing subclasses to implement specific details. In enterprise software, they enable code reuse and enforce consistency across related components. For instance, an abstract `Employee` class can define methods like `calculateSalary()` and `trackAttendance()`, which are customized in subclasses like `Manager` and `Intern`. Abstract classes simplify design by capturing common functionalities, ensuring that all derived classes adhere to a predefined interface. This approach supports scalability and maintainability, key requirements in enterprise environments.

33. Explain the concept of object responsibility and its role in cohesive system design.
Answer: Object responsibility refers to the specific tasks or roles assigned to an object within a system. Clearly defining responsibilities ensures that each object focuses on a single purpose, promoting high cohesion. For example, a `PaymentProcessor` object should only handle payment logic, not user authentication or report generation. Assigning appropriate responsibilities simplifies system design, enhances readability, and makes components more

reusable. In OOAD, responsibility-driven design supports maintainability and minimizes the risk of tightly coupled systems that are difficult to modify or extend.

34. Evaluate the importance of loose coupling in distributed software systems.
Answer: Loose coupling is critical in distributed systems because it allows individual components to function independently and interact through well-defined interfaces. This design principle enables developers to modify, scale, or replace one component without affecting others, which is essential in large, dynamic environments like cloud-based applications. Loose coupling also enhances fault isolation, as failures in one module are less likely to propagate system-wide. In OOAD, loose coupling is achieved using techniques such as dependency injection, interfaces, and encapsulation, resulting in more flexible, resilient, and maintainable distributed systems.

35. Discuss the challenges and solutions in applying inheritance in deep hierarchies.
Answer: Deep inheritance hierarchies can introduce challenges such as increased complexity, tight coupling between parent and child classes, and difficulty understanding inherited behaviors. Changes in a base class may unintentionally affect multiple subclasses, leading to fragile designs. Solutions include limiting hierarchy depth, favoring composition over inheritance when appropriate, and applying design patterns like Strategy or Decorator for dynamic behavior changes. Careful analysis during OOAD ensures that inheritance is used judiciously to promote code reuse while avoiding the pitfalls of overly rigid class structures.

36. Assess how UML component diagrams aid in managing software complexity.
Answer: UML component diagrams provide a high-level view of software systems by illustrating how components interact and depend on each other. They help manage complexity by breaking the system into modular units, making it easier to understand, develop, and maintain. These diagrams are particularly useful in large-scale projects, where they show how individual modules fit into the overall architecture. Component diagrams also facilitate parallel development by clarifying dependencies and interfaces between components, enabling teams to work independently on different parts of the system.

37. Explain the concept of delegation and its advantages in OOAD.
Answer: Delegation is a design principle where an object passes responsibility for a specific task to another object, allowing for greater flexibility and code reuse. Instead of inheriting behavior, an object uses a helper or delegate to perform certain actions. For example, a `Printer` object might delegate formatting responsibilities to a `Formatter` object. Delegation promotes loose coupling by separating concerns and making it easier to swap out or modify delegated behaviors without affecting the core object. This approach supports dynamic behavior composition and simplifies maintenance in complex systems.

38. Evaluate the benefits of using the Observer pattern in event-driven systems.
Answer: The Observer pattern facilitates communication in event-driven systems by establishing a one-to-many dependency between objects. When the state of a subject changes, all registered observers are notified automatically. This pattern is beneficial in systems like user interfaces, where changes in data models must update multiple views simultaneously. It promotes loose coupling, as subjects and observers interact through well-defined interfaces, allowing developers to add or remove observers dynamically. The Observer pattern enhances scalability and maintainability, making it a cornerstone of reactive programming and real-time applications.

39. Discuss how object-oriented design supports secure software development.
Answer: Object-oriented design supports secure software development through encapsulation, modularity, and controlled access to sensitive data. Encapsulation restricts direct access to critical attributes, ensuring that interactions occur only through validated methods. Modular design isolates components, limiting the scope of potential vulnerabilities. Principles like least privilege are enforced through visibility modifiers and secure interfaces. Additionally, design patterns such as Proxy and Decorator can be used to implement security features like authentication and access control. OOAD provides a robust foundation for building secure, maintainable software systems.

40. Analyze the impact of design patterns on system scalability and maintainability.
Answer: Design patterns provide reusable solutions to common design challenges, promoting system scalability and

maintainability. Patterns like Singleton ensure efficient resource management, while Factory and Abstract Factory simplify object creation in large systems. Observer and Strategy patterns enable dynamic behavior changes, supporting system flexibility as requirements evolve. By standardizing solutions, design patterns improve code readability and facilitate collaboration among developers. They also reduce development time and errors, making systems easier to extend and maintain in response to new business needs.

41. Explain the advantages of modeling relationships using aggregation and composition in UML.
Answer: Aggregation and composition model "has-a" relationships in UML, providing clarity in how objects relate. Aggregation represents a weak relationship where parts can exist independently of the whole, such as a `Library` and `Books`. Composition represents a strong relationship where parts depend on the whole for their lifecycle, like a `House` and its `Rooms`. Using these relationships helps designers model systems accurately, supporting maintainability and reusability. They clarify ownership and dependencies, ensuring systems reflect real-world constraints and promoting robust object-oriented designs.

42. Evaluate the role of high cohesion in object-oriented software architecture.
Answer: High cohesion ensures that each class or module in an object-oriented system focuses on a single, well-defined responsibility. This design principle simplifies understanding, testing, and maintenance by keeping related functionalities together. Highly cohesive components are easier to reuse and modify without unintended side effects. In contrast, low cohesion often leads to scattered responsibilities and tightly coupled systems that are fragile and difficult to maintain. OOAD emphasizes high cohesion to build robust, modular architectures that scale effectively with system complexity.

43. Discuss the significance of object-oriented design in agile software development.
Answer: Object-oriented design aligns closely with agile software development by promoting modularity, flexibility, and iterative design. Encapsulation allows teams to make localized changes without disrupting the entire system. Inheritance and polymorphism enable incremental enhancements and support refactoring. OOAD's use of UML diagrams provides lightweight documentation that facilitates communication between developers and stakeholders. This synergy allows agile teams to deliver working software quickly, respond to changing requirements, and maintain high-quality code through continuous integration and delivery practices.

44. Analyze the benefits of applying the Proxy pattern in networked applications.
Answer: The Proxy pattern acts as a surrogate for another object, controlling access to it. In networked applications, proxies are useful for managing resource-intensive operations like database connections, caching, or security checks. For example, a proxy can handle authentication before granting access to a server resource. This pattern reduces system load by optimizing network usage and providing centralized control over resource access. Proxies enhance security, improve performance, and support scalability in distributed systems, making them valuable in client-server architectures and cloud-based applications.

45. Explain how object-oriented decomposition facilitates modular software design.
Answer: Object-oriented decomposition breaks a system into smaller, manageable components based on real-world entities. Each component encapsulates its data and behavior, promoting modular design. This approach simplifies development by allowing teams to focus on individual modules, such as user management or payment processing, independently. Encapsulation ensures that changes within a module do not affect others, reducing integration risks. Object-oriented decomposition supports reusability and scalability, enabling systems to evolve over time while maintaining a clean and organized architecture.

46. Assess how object-oriented design supports dynamic system behavior through runtime binding.
Answer: Object-oriented design supports dynamic behavior through runtime binding, where method calls are resolved at execution rather than compile time. This enables polymorphism, allowing different objects to respond to the same message in context-specific ways. For example, a `draw()` method call on a `Shape` reference invokes the appropriate implementation for a `Circle` or `Rectangle` at runtime. Runtime binding allows systems to adapt behavior dynamically, supporting flexible and extensible designs. It is particularly useful in plugin-based architectures and systems requiring runtime adaptability.

47. Discuss the importance of object immutability in multi-threaded systems.
Answer: Object immutability ensures that once an object is created, its state cannot be modified. This property is critical in multi-threaded systems because immutable objects are inherently thread-safe, eliminating the need for synchronization. For example, Java's `String` class is immutable, preventing issues like race conditions during concurrent access. Immutability simplifies debugging, enhances system stability, and supports functional programming practices in object-oriented designs. However, excessive use of immutability may lead to increased memory usage due to frequent object creation.

48. Evaluate the advantages of applying the Adapter pattern in integrating legacy systems.
Answer: The Adapter pattern enables new systems to work with legacy systems by converting incompatible interfaces into compatible ones. This pattern allows developers to integrate modern components without modifying existing legacy code. For example, an adapter can translate data formats or communication protocols between a new API and an old database system. Applying the Adapter pattern extends the lifespan of legacy systems, supports gradual migration to newer technologies, and reduces development costs by avoiding complete system rewrites.

49. Explain how UML sequence diagrams assist in identifying potential system bottlenecks.
Answer: UML sequence diagrams model the flow of messages between objects over time, revealing the order and dependencies of operations. By analyzing these diagrams, developers can identify potential bottlenecks, such as excessive calls to a particular object or delays in response times. This insight supports optimization efforts, such as caching frequently accessed data or redesigning workflows for efficiency. Sequence diagrams are particularly useful in performance-critical applications like e-commerce platforms, where understanding object interactions is key to delivering responsive user experiences.

50. Analyze how OOAD principles support building secure and scalable APIs.
Answer: OOAD principles like encapsulation, modularity, and loose coupling are essential for building secure and scalable APIs. Encapsulation restricts direct access to sensitive data, exposing only necessary endpoints. Modularity allows APIs to be developed, tested, and scaled independently. Polymorphism supports flexible API designs that handle diverse input types and evolve over time without breaking backward compatibility. Design patterns like Proxy and Decorator add layers of security and logging around API calls. Together, these principles ensure APIs are robust, adaptable, and capable of handling large volumes of requests securely.

51. Explain how object-oriented design supports the development of scalable e-commerce platforms.
Answer: Object-oriented design supports scalable e-commerce platforms by emphasizing modularity, reusability, and abstraction. Components such as product catalogs, payment gateways, and user profiles are modeled as independent objects that encapsulate data and behavior. This modular architecture allows each component to scale horizontally or vertically based on demand. For instance, the `OrderProcessor` class can handle transactions independently of the `InventoryManager` class. Polymorphism allows the integration of new payment methods without altering existing logic. Design patterns like Singleton and Factory further simplify resource management and object creation, ensuring e-commerce platforms remain flexible and capable of handling high traffic volumes.

52. Assess the role of the Strategy pattern in developing customizable applications.
Answer: The Strategy pattern enables customizable applications by defining a family of algorithms and making them interchangeable at runtime. For instance, in a sorting application, different sorting algorithms like QuickSort, MergeSort, or BubbleSort can be implemented as separate strategies. The context class delegates the sorting task to a chosen strategy, allowing the behavior to change dynamically based on user preferences or data types. This approach promotes flexibility, reduces code duplication, and adheres to the Open/Closed Principle, enabling developers to add new strategies without modifying existing code.

53. Discuss how UML class diagrams aid in maintaining large enterprise software systems.
Answer: UML class diagrams provide a visual representation of the system's static structure, showing classes, attributes, methods, and relationships. In large enterprise systems, these diagrams serve as critical documentation, helping developers understand complex hierarchies and dependencies. Class diagrams make it easier to identify reusable components, plan modifications, and ensure that changes do not introduce unintended side effects. They also

support onboarding new team members by offering a clear overview of the system architecture. This visual clarity reduces maintenance effort and promotes consistency across enterprise software.

54. Evaluate the benefits of applying object-oriented principles in IoT system development.
Answer: Object-oriented principles benefit IoT systems by modeling devices as objects with encapsulated data and behaviors. Encapsulation isolates each device's logic, ensuring that changes in one component do not affect others. Polymorphism allows different device types to interact through common interfaces, simplifying the integration of new sensors or actuators. Inheritance supports the creation of device hierarchies, where shared functionalities are defined in base classes. Design patterns like Observer enable efficient event handling in IoT networks. This modular approach ensures IoT systems are scalable, maintainable, and adaptable to evolving technologies.

55. Explain how object-oriented testing addresses the unique challenges of OOAD systems.
Answer: Object-oriented testing addresses challenges such as encapsulation, inheritance, and polymorphism by focusing on class-level and integration-level tests. Unit tests validate individual methods and ensure encapsulated data behaves correctly under various scenarios. Polymorphism requires careful testing to ensure overridden methods in subclasses maintain expected behavior. Inheritance hierarchies are tested using techniques like Liskov Substitution Principle validation. Mock objects and stubs facilitate testing object collaborations without relying on complex dependencies. By addressing these challenges, object-oriented testing ensures systems remain robust and reliable.

56. Analyze the importance of loose coupling in supporting API-based architectures.
Answer: Loose coupling is essential in API-based architectures because it ensures that services interact through well-defined contracts without depending on internal implementations. This design allows developers to update, replace, or scale individual services independently, supporting rapid development cycles and system flexibility. Loose coupling also facilitates third-party integrations, as APIs expose only necessary endpoints while hiding underlying complexities. In OOAD, principles like dependency injection and design patterns such as Facade promote loose coupling, ensuring APIs remain robust and adaptable in dynamic business environments.

57. Discuss the significance of high cohesion in distributed software systems.
Answer: High cohesion ensures that each component in a distributed software system focuses on a single, well-defined responsibility. This clarity simplifies understanding, debugging, and maintenance, especially when components are deployed across multiple servers. Highly cohesive modules are easier to scale independently, as their functionality does not overlap with other components. In OOAD, high cohesion complements loose coupling, resulting in systems that are both modular and resilient. This design principle is crucial for maintaining performance and reliability in complex distributed architectures like cloud-based applications.

58. Evaluate how the Decorator pattern enhances flexibility in UI component design.
Answer: The Decorator pattern enhances flexibility in UI component design by allowing behaviors to be added dynamically to individual components without altering their structure. For instance, in a GUI system, a basic `TextBox` can be decorated with features like borders, scrollbars, or color themes. Each decorator wraps the base component, extending its functionality while preserving its interface. This approach adheres to the Open/Closed Principle, enabling developers to introduce new features without modifying existing code. The Decorator pattern supports highly customizable and reusable UI designs, ideal for modern user-centric applications.

59. Explain how object-oriented middleware supports interoperability in heterogeneous environments.
Answer: Object-oriented middleware enables interoperability by abstracting communication complexities in heterogeneous environments where systems use different platforms, programming languages, or protocols. Middleware technologies like CORBA or Java RMI allow distributed objects to interact seamlessly by handling tasks such as data serialization, object referencing, and message routing. This abstraction lets developers focus on business logic instead of network details. Middleware also provides services like transaction management and security, ensuring consistent and reliable interactions across diverse systems.

60. Analyze the role of UML sequence diagrams in designing event-driven architectures.
Answer: UML sequence diagrams are instrumental in designing event-driven architectures as they illustrate the flow of messages between objects over time. These diagrams show how events trigger specific actions and how objects

collaborate to process them. For example, in a stock trading application, a sequence diagram can model how a price update event propagates through the system to notify users and execute orders. Sequence diagrams help identify potential delays, bottlenecks, and race conditions, enabling developers to design efficient and reliable event-driven systems.

61. Assess the advantages of applying the Composite pattern in hierarchical data structures.
Answer: The Composite pattern simplifies working with hierarchical data structures by allowing clients to treat individual objects and compositions uniformly. For example, in a file system, both files and directories can implement a common interface, enabling operations like `display()` or `delete()` to work recursively. This design promotes flexibility and simplifies client code by hiding the complexity of traversing hierarchies. The Composite pattern supports scalability and maintainability, making it ideal for applications like UI frameworks, organizational charts, and document processing systems.

62. Discuss how object-oriented principles contribute to software reusability.
Answer: Object-oriented principles like encapsulation, inheritance, and polymorphism promote software reusability by enabling developers to create modular, self-contained components. Encapsulation isolates functionality, allowing classes to be reused without exposing internal details. Inheritance facilitates extending existing classes, while polymorphism enables generic interfaces for interacting with diverse object types. Design patterns further standardize reusable solutions for common problems. Together, these principles reduce development time, improve consistency, and support the creation of libraries and frameworks that can be applied across multiple projects.

63. Explain how dependency inversion supports flexible system design in OOAD.
Answer: Dependency inversion supports flexible system design by encouraging high-level modules to depend on abstractions rather than concrete implementations. This approach allows developers to change or replace low-level modules without affecting higher-level logic. For example, a payment processing system can depend on a `PaymentGateway` interface, enabling easy integration of new providers like Stripe or PayPal. Dependency inversion reduces coupling, simplifies testing with mock objects, and promotes scalability by supporting interchangeable components. It is a key principle for achieving robust and adaptable object-oriented systems.

64. Analyze the benefits of applying the Command pattern in task scheduling systems.
Answer: The Command pattern encapsulates requests as objects, allowing tasks to be queued, logged, or undone in scheduling systems. Each command object implements an execute() method, enabling uniform handling of diverse operations. For example, in a job scheduler, tasks like sending emails or generating reports can be treated as command objects and executed dynamically based on schedules or priorities. This pattern simplifies task management, supports undo/redo functionality, and enhances system extensibility by allowing new commands to be added without modifying existing code.

65. Discuss how object-oriented design supports version control in large projects.
Answer: Object-oriented design supports version control by promoting modular architectures where components can evolve independently. Encapsulation and loose coupling reduce the impact of changes, enabling teams to update specific modules without affecting others. Clear class and interface definitions make it easier to track changes, resolve conflicts, and manage dependencies in version control systems like Git. OOAD also complements branching strategies by allowing parallel development on different system parts. This structured approach streamlines collaboration in large, distributed teams.

66. Evaluate the importance of modeling object relationships in UML for database design.
Answer: Modeling object relationships in UML is crucial for translating object-oriented designs into effective database schemas. Associations, aggregations, and compositions in UML diagrams guide the creation of foreign keys and relational mappings in databases. For instance, a one-to-many relationship in UML informs the design of parent-child tables in a relational database. These models ensure data integrity, support efficient queries, and align database structures with application logic. In OOAD, tools like Object-Relational Mapping (ORM) frameworks rely on these relationships for seamless data persistence.

67. Explain how OOAD supports DevOps practices in modern software development.
Answer: OOAD supports DevOps practices by emphasizing modularity, reusability, and clear system boundaries. Modular designs facilitate continuous integration and delivery, as components can be tested and deployed independently. Encapsulation ensures predictable behavior, simplifying automated testing pipelines. Object-oriented principles align well with containerization technologies like Docker, where services encapsulate functionality and dependencies. UML diagrams aid in planning infrastructure and deployment strategies. Together, these practices enable faster development cycles, improved collaboration, and more reliable software releases.

68. Discuss how object-oriented design simplifies internationalization and localization in software.
Answer: Object-oriented design simplifies internationalization and localization by encapsulating language-specific content in dedicated classes or resource bundles. For instance, a `LanguageManager` class can handle retrieving localized strings, dates, and currency formats. Polymorphism supports region-specific behaviors, such as different tax calculations for various countries. This modular approach ensures that changes to localization logic do not affect core system functionalities. OOAD's focus on abstraction and separation of concerns enables developers to add new languages or regions with minimal code modifications.

69. Assess the advantages of applying the Mediator pattern in GUI applications.
Answer: The Mediator pattern centralizes communication between GUI components, reducing direct dependencies and simplifying component interactions. In a dialog box, for example, the mediator coordinates actions between text fields, buttons, and drop-down menus. This approach prevents tightly coupled components, making the GUI more maintainable and extensible. The Mediator pattern enhances reusability by allowing components to be used in different contexts without modification. It also supports dynamic behavior changes, as developers can modify interaction logic by updating the mediator rather than altering individual components.

70. Analyze how object-oriented principles support fault tolerance in distributed systems.
Answer: Object-oriented principles support fault tolerance in distributed systems by promoting modular and encapsulated designs that isolate failures. Encapsulation ensures that errors in one module do not propagate to others. Design patterns like Proxy can implement retry mechanisms or fallback strategies for network failures. Polymorphism allows systems to switch between redundant components seamlessly. By modeling resilient objects and interactions, OOAD enables distributed systems to detect, contain, and recover from faults effectively, ensuring consistent performance even in adverse conditions.

71. Explain how object-oriented design facilitates the creation of modular cloud-based applications.
Answer: Object-oriented design facilitates modular cloud-based applications by structuring systems as collections of loosely coupled and highly cohesive components. Each module, represented as a class or object, encapsulates its data and behavior, enabling independent deployment and scaling in a cloud environment. This modularity aligns perfectly with microservices architecture, where each service represents a specific domain logic. Polymorphism supports integration with different cloud APIs, and design patterns such as Singleton manage shared resources effectively. This approach ensures flexibility, maintainability, and scalability, which are crucial for modern applications running in distributed cloud infrastructures.

72. Assess the advantages of applying the Builder pattern in complex object creation.
Answer: The Builder pattern simplifies the creation of complex objects by separating the construction process from the object's representation. This design allows developers to build objects step-by-step with different configurations. For instance, in a document generator application, the Builder can create various formats such as PDFs or HTML by following the same construction process. Advantages include improved code readability, reusability of construction logic, and easier maintenance. The Builder pattern is especially useful when objects require many optional parameters or when different representations of the same object are needed.

73. Discuss the importance of object collaboration in use case implementation.
Answer: Object collaboration is vital in implementing use cases because it defines how multiple objects interact to fulfill a system's functional requirements. Each object plays a specific role and communicates through message passing to achieve a common goal. For instance, in an online shopping use case, `Customer`, `ShoppingCart`, `OrderProcessor`, and `PaymentGateway` objects collaborate to complete a purchase. Understanding these

interactions ensures that responsibilities are distributed appropriately, enhancing system cohesion and reducing coupling. UML sequence and collaboration diagrams help visualize and validate these interactions during the design phase.

74. Analyze how object-oriented design supports continuous integration and delivery pipelines.
Answer: Object-oriented design supports continuous integration (CI) and delivery (CD) by promoting modularity, encapsulation, and reusable components. Modular systems allow developers to test and deploy individual parts without impacting the entire application. Encapsulation ensures that changes are localized, minimizing conflicts during integration. Object-oriented principles facilitate automated unit testing, as classes and methods can be tested independently. CI/CD pipelines benefit from this structure because they can quickly build, test, and deploy incremental changes, enabling rapid iteration and reducing deployment risks in agile development environments.

75. Explain the concept of object persistence and its role in data-intensive applications.
Answer: Object persistence ensures that the state of an object can be stored and retrieved across program executions. In data-intensive applications, this allows critical data like user profiles, transactions, or configurations to remain intact even after a system restart. Object-Relational Mapping (ORM) frameworks such as Hibernate bridge the gap between object-oriented models and relational databases, automating data persistence. This approach simplifies application logic, reduces boilerplate code, and ensures consistency between in-memory objects and stored data. Persistence is critical for maintaining reliability and user trust in systems that manage large volumes of data.

76. Evaluate how the Facade pattern simplifies system interactions for end users and developers.
Answer: The Facade pattern provides a unified interface to a complex subsystem, simplifying interactions for both end users and developers. It hides the complexity of multiple underlying classes by offering a single entry point for operations. For example, in a banking application, a `BankFacade` class can manage interactions with accounts, loans, and notifications, making it easier for developers to perform high-level operations without dealing with intricate details. This pattern promotes loose coupling, improves maintainability, and enhances usability by streamlining system access.

77. Discuss how object-oriented principles help design testable and maintainable APIs.
Answer: Object-oriented principles like encapsulation, abstraction, and polymorphism help design APIs that are both testable and maintainable. Encapsulation ensures that API internals remain hidden, exposing only necessary endpoints for clients. Abstraction defines clear contracts through interfaces, enabling developers to test API behavior independently of implementations. Polymorphism allows APIs to handle various data types or request formats dynamically. Design patterns such as Adapter and Proxy further enhance testability by supporting mock implementations and controlled access during testing. Together, these principles promote robust APIs that evolve easily over time.

78. Analyze the role of high cohesion in building reliable healthcare management systems.
Answer: High cohesion ensures that each module in a healthcare management system has a single, well-defined responsibility, such as patient record management or appointment scheduling. This clarity reduces system complexity, simplifies debugging, and improves reliability. For example, changes to the billing module will not inadvertently affect patient data handling. High cohesion also facilitates compliance with healthcare standards like HIPAA by isolating sensitive data processing. In OOAD, designing cohesive classes ensures that healthcare systems remain robust, maintainable, and secure while supporting critical workflows.

79. Explain how UML object diagrams support debugging and testing activities.
Answer: UML object diagrams provide snapshots of system instances and their relationships at a specific point in time. They are invaluable during debugging and testing because they show the actual configuration of objects and data during execution. For instance, developers can use object diagrams to verify whether objects are correctly instantiated and whether relationships such as associations or aggregations are properly established. These diagrams help identify logical errors, unintended dependencies, or incorrect data flows, supporting faster issue resolution and more effective system validation.

80. Assess the advantages of applying the Prototype pattern in systems requiring dynamic object creation.
Answer: The Prototype pattern enables dynamic object creation by cloning existing objects instead of instantiating new ones from scratch. This is advantageous in systems where object creation is resource-intensive or where objects require complex initialization. For example, in a graphics application, prototypes of shapes can be cloned and customized without reloading configuration data. The Prototype pattern supports flexibility, reduces object creation overhead, and simplifies the addition of new object types at runtime. It is especially useful in scenarios involving frequent object creation or undo operations.

81. Discuss how object-oriented design supports secure transaction management in financial systems.
Answer: Object-oriented design supports secure transaction management by encapsulating sensitive operations within well-defined classes and controlling access through secure interfaces. For instance, a `TransactionManager` class can validate inputs, enforce authorization, and ensure atomicity of transactions. Encapsulation isolates transaction logic, preventing unauthorized access or unintended data manipulation. Design patterns like Proxy can add layers of security, such as encryption and authentication, around transaction processes. OOAD ensures financial systems maintain data integrity, confidentiality, and compliance with regulatory standards like PCI DSS.

82. Explain how UML activity diagrams assist in process optimization.
Answer: UML activity diagrams visually represent workflows, decision points, and parallel activities, making them powerful tools for process optimization. They allow stakeholders to identify inefficiencies, redundant steps, and bottlenecks in business processes. For example, in a supply chain management system, activity diagrams can help streamline order processing by highlighting delays in approvals or handoffs. Optimizing these workflows ensures faster response times and improved resource utilization. Activity diagrams also facilitate collaboration between technical and non-technical teams during system analysis and design.

83. Evaluate the use of object-oriented design in supporting disaster recovery planning.
Answer: Object-oriented design supports disaster recovery planning by promoting modularity and encapsulation. Each module can be independently backed up, restored, or migrated, ensuring minimal disruption in case of system failure. Encapsulation isolates critical data and logic, enabling targeted recovery efforts. Design patterns like Singleton can manage configuration settings consistently across primary and backup systems. OOAD's modular architecture aligns well with distributed systems, allowing developers to implement failover strategies and redundant components that ensure business continuity during disasters.

84. Discuss how the Adapter pattern enables system interoperability in legacy systems.
Answer: The Adapter pattern enables interoperability by bridging the gap between incompatible interfaces of legacy systems and modern applications. It acts as a translator, allowing new components to interact with older ones without modifying legacy code. For instance, an adapter can convert API calls from a modern frontend to match the protocol of an outdated backend service. This approach reduces redevelopment costs, supports gradual modernization, and extends the lifespan of legacy systems while enabling integration with contemporary technologies.

85. Analyze how object-oriented principles help manage complexity in AI-driven systems.
Answer: Object-oriented principles manage complexity in AI-driven systems by encapsulating data processing and decision-making logic within modular components. For instance, a `ModelTrainer` class can handle training operations independently of a `DataPreprocessor` class. Polymorphism supports integrating different AI models dynamically, and inheritance allows shared functionalities like data validation to be reused across multiple components. This modularity simplifies debugging, testing, and updating AI algorithms while ensuring that system changes remain localized and manageable.

86. Explain how the Observer pattern supports real-time data updates in monitoring systems.
Answer: The Observer pattern supports real-time updates by allowing monitoring systems to automatically notify subscribed components when data changes. For example, in a weather monitoring application, sensors (subjects) can notify display units (observers) whenever temperature or humidity levels change. This design ensures that observers always have the latest information without polling for updates. The Observer pattern promotes loose coupling, enabling dynamic addition or removal of observers and supporting scalability in systems that require frequent, real-time data propagation.

87. Discuss the role of encapsulation in implementing business rules securely.
Answer: Encapsulation secures business rule implementation by restricting direct access to critical data and enforcing validations through controlled interfaces. For example, in a payroll system, salary calculations and tax deductions can be encapsulated within specific classes, preventing external components from bypassing rules. This approach ensures data integrity and compliance with organizational policies. Encapsulation also simplifies auditing and debugging by localizing rule logic, making it easier to track changes and ensure secure and predictable system behavior.

88. Assess how object-oriented design supports resource optimization in embedded systems.
Answer: Object-oriented design supports resource optimization in embedded systems by promoting modularity and code reuse. Encapsulation ensures efficient memory management by isolating components and controlling data access. Design patterns like Object Pooling and Flyweight help minimize resource consumption by reusing objects and sharing common data. Polymorphism enables flexible behavior adjustments without duplicating code, which is crucial in systems with limited processing power and storage. OOAD provides a structured approach to designing lightweight, efficient embedded applications.

89. Explain how UML state diagrams aid in modeling user interactions for mobile applications.
Answer: UML state diagrams model user interactions by illustrating how application states change in response to events, such as button clicks or gestures. In mobile applications, state diagrams help designers visualize transitions between screens (e.g., login, dashboard, settings) and identify edge cases like invalid inputs or session timeouts. This modeling ensures predictable behavior and enhances user experience by preventing inconsistent states. State diagrams are invaluable for validating workflows and ensuring robust navigation in complex mobile app designs.

90. Analyze the significance of applying SOLID principles in object-oriented software design.
Answer: Applying SOLID principles in object-oriented software design ensures systems are modular, maintainable, and scalable. The Single Responsibility Principle keeps classes focused, enhancing cohesion and simplifying testing. The Open/Closed Principle allows systems to be extended without modifying existing code. Liskov Substitution, Interface Segregation, and Dependency Inversion further promote flexibility and loose coupling. Together, these principles reduce technical debt, prevent code fragility, and make systems easier to evolve as requirements change. SOLID principles form the foundation of robust, high-quality object-oriented software architectures.

111. Analyze how the Bridge pattern supports the separation of abstraction and implementation in software systems.
Answer: The Bridge pattern promotes the separation of abstraction and implementation by allowing them to vary independently. It achieves this by using composition instead of inheritance, where an abstraction maintains a reference to an implementation object. For example, in a graphics library, the `Shape` abstraction can reference different rendering implementations like `OpenGLRenderer` or `DirectXRenderer`. This design allows developers to extend abstractions and implementations without affecting each other. The Bridge pattern enhances flexibility, reduces code duplication, and supports systems that require multiple dimensions of variability.

112. Discuss the importance of UML interaction diagrams in designing responsive user interfaces.
Answer: UML interaction diagrams, such as sequence and communication diagrams, play a crucial role in designing responsive user interfaces (UI). They model dynamic interactions between UI components and backend services, visualizing message flows and event handling. For instance, a sequence diagram can illustrate how a button click triggers a series of actions leading to a UI update. This helps identify potential delays, race conditions, or unnecessary dependencies. By analyzing these diagrams, designers can optimize workflows and ensure that UIs remain responsive and user-friendly, even under high loads or complex interactions.

113. Explain how object-oriented principles simplify multi-platform software development.
Answer: Object-oriented principles simplify multi-platform development by promoting abstraction, encapsulation, and modularity. Platform-specific details are encapsulated within dedicated classes, while common logic resides in shared components. For instance, a `FileManager` interface can have platform-specific implementations for Windows, Linux, and macOS. Polymorphism ensures that the system can use these implementations interchangeably at runtime. This structure enables developers to maintain a single codebase with minimal duplication, simplifying

updates and ensuring consistency across platforms. OOAD supports scalability and efficiency in building applications for diverse environments.

114. Evaluate the advantages of using the Singleton pattern in configuration management.
Answer: The Singleton pattern is advantageous in configuration management because it ensures a single, globally accessible instance of a configuration object throughout the application's lifecycle. This centralization prevents inconsistencies in accessing application settings like database connections, API keys, or user preferences. Singleton also supports lazy initialization, allowing configuration data to load only when required, optimizing resource usage. However, care must be taken in multi-threaded environments to implement thread-safe Singletons. This pattern is essential for maintaining stability and consistency in systems where configuration plays a critical role.

115. Discuss how object-oriented design enhances software portability across hardware architectures.
Answer: Object-oriented design enhances portability by isolating hardware-specific details within modular, encapsulated components. Abstraction layers provide a consistent interface to the application, while platform-dependent code is implemented in interchangeable modules. For example, in a graphics engine, rendering logic can be abstracted from hardware APIs, allowing the system to switch between OpenGL and DirectX implementations seamlessly. This design reduces platform lock-in and simplifies adapting software to new hardware architectures, enabling wider deployment and longer software lifecycles.

116. Analyze how the Visitor pattern simplifies operations on complex object structures.
Answer: The Visitor pattern simplifies operations on complex object structures by separating algorithms from the objects they operate on. It allows adding new behaviors without modifying the existing class hierarchy. For example, in a file system, a `Visitor` can traverse directories and perform operations like size calculation or virus scanning without altering `File` and `Directory` classes. This approach adheres to the Open/Closed Principle and supports flexibility when working with heterogeneous object structures. The Visitor pattern is particularly effective in compiler design and data analytics applications.

117. Explain how object-oriented design supports secure data sharing in collaborative systems.
Answer: Object-oriented design supports secure data sharing in collaborative systems by encapsulating sensitive operations within secure components and defining clear access control mechanisms. Classes handling shared data can enforce validation and authentication, ensuring only authorized users can perform specific actions. Design patterns like Proxy and Decorator can add security layers such as encryption and logging around data access. Modular designs allow secure APIs for sharing data between components or external systems while protecting core business logic. OOAD ensures that collaborative systems maintain confidentiality and integrity in multi-user environments.

118. Evaluate how the State pattern supports dynamic behavior in context-aware applications.
Answer: The State pattern supports dynamic behavior in context-aware applications by allowing an object to change its behavior based on its internal state. Each state is represented as a separate class, and the context object delegates behavior to the current state. For instance, in a media player, states like Playing, Paused, and Stopped define different responses to user inputs. This design simplifies code by avoiding complex conditional logic and supports systems where behavior must adapt in real time to environmental changes, such as mobile or IoT applications.

119. Discuss how object-oriented principles enable better versioning and backward compatibility in APIs.
Answer: Object-oriented principles enable better versioning and backward compatibility by promoting modularity and abstraction. Interfaces define clear contracts that remain stable even as implementations evolve. Polymorphism allows new API versions to coexist with older ones, ensuring that legacy clients continue to function. Encapsulation hides implementation details, allowing internal changes without affecting external consumers. Design patterns like Adapter can bridge old and new API formats, supporting smooth migrations. OOAD's emphasis on reusable and flexible designs ensures APIs remain robust and adaptable over time.

120. Explain the role of UML activity diagrams in automating business workflows.
Answer: UML activity diagrams play a pivotal role in automating business workflows by modeling the flow of activities, decisions, and parallel processes. They provide a clear visual representation of how tasks progress and how exceptions are handled. For example, in an insurance claim process, activity diagrams can outline steps from claim

submission to approval and payment. These diagrams guide the development of workflow engines and business process automation tools, ensuring accuracy and efficiency. They also help stakeholders validate processes before implementation, reducing errors and optimizing operations.

121. Analyze how object-oriented design supports data abstraction in machine learning systems.
Answer: Object-oriented design supports data abstraction in machine learning systems by encapsulating data preprocessing, model training, and prediction logic within dedicated components. Abstraction layers hide complexities like feature engineering or data storage, exposing only necessary methods for higher-level operations. For example, a `Model` interface can define train() and predict() methods, while specific algorithms like DecisionTree or NeuralNetwork implement them. This design promotes modularity, allowing developers to swap models or preprocessing techniques without altering core workflows, enabling experimentation and rapid innovation.

122. Discuss the significance of object-oriented design in building fault-tolerant IoT networks.
Answer: Object-oriented design is significant in fault-tolerant IoT networks because it promotes modular, resilient architectures. Each device or sensor is modeled as an independent object with encapsulated logic, enabling localized error handling and recovery. Design patterns like Observer support real-time updates and dynamic reconfiguration when nodes fail. Encapsulation ensures that failures in one component do not cascade through the system. OOAD enables redundancy strategies, such as duplicate objects or failover mechanisms, ensuring continuous operation in environments where device reliability is critical.

123. Evaluate how the Abstract Factory pattern supports platform independence in cross-platform applications.
Answer: The Abstract Factory pattern supports platform independence by providing a way to create families of related objects without specifying their concrete classes. It encapsulates the creation logic, allowing applications to generate platform-specific components dynamically. For example, in a GUI library, an abstract factory can produce Windows, macOS, or Linux-specific widgets while presenting a unified interface to the application. This design enables developers to maintain a single codebase while supporting multiple platforms, simplifying deployment and ensuring consistent behavior across environments.

124. Explain how object-oriented principles enhance the testability of distributed applications.
Answer: Object-oriented principles enhance testability by creating modular and loosely coupled systems where components can be tested independently. Encapsulation isolates logic within classes, simplifying unit testing. Polymorphism supports mocking and stubbing during integration tests, enabling developers to simulate distributed services. Design patterns like Dependency Injection make it easy to swap real implementations with test doubles. OOAD's emphasis on clear interfaces and reusable components ensures that distributed applications remain testable even as they grow in complexity, supporting reliable deployments.

125. Discuss how object-oriented design contributes to the longevity and adaptability of enterprise software.
Answer: Object-oriented design contributes to the longevity and adaptability of enterprise software by promoting modularity, reusability, and flexibility. Encapsulation isolates changes, enabling safe updates and extensions without disrupting core functionalities. Inheritance supports consistent enhancements across related components, while polymorphism allows systems to adapt dynamically to new business requirements. Design patterns provide proven solutions for common challenges, ensuring scalable and maintainable architectures. OOAD helps enterprises evolve their software in response to market changes and technological advancements, extending its usable lifespan and reducing redevelopment costs.

126. Explain how object-oriented design supports continuous monitoring in enterprise applications.
Answer: Object-oriented design supports continuous monitoring in enterprise applications by structuring monitoring functionality into modular and reusable components. Encapsulation ensures that metrics collection, logging, and alerting logic are isolated within dedicated classes such as `Monitor` or `Logger`. Design patterns like Observer allow monitoring systems to react dynamically to state changes in critical objects, enabling real-time updates. Polymorphism supports integration with various monitoring tools and APIs without altering core application logic. This modular approach simplifies adding new monitoring capabilities and ensures enterprise systems remain reliable and maintainable under continuous supervision.

127. Analyze how the Decorator pattern enhances extensibility in analytics dashboards.
Answer: The Decorator pattern enhances extensibility in analytics dashboards by allowing additional functionalities, such as filters, themes, or visualization options, to be added dynamically. Instead of modifying core components like charts or tables, decorators wrap these components, extending their behavior. For example, a base `Chart` class can be decorated with zooming or export capabilities as needed. This approach adheres to the Open/Closed Principle, enabling new features to be introduced without altering existing code. It supports highly customizable dashboards that adapt easily to evolving user requirements in enterprise analytics systems.

128. Discuss the role of object-oriented principles in minimizing technical debt.
Answer: Object-oriented principles minimize technical debt by promoting clean, modular designs that are easier to understand, maintain, and extend. Encapsulation isolates responsibilities, reducing the risk of unintended side effects during changes. Inheritance promotes code reuse, preventing duplication and inconsistencies. Polymorphism supports flexible designs that adapt to new requirements without breaking existing functionality. By adhering to these principles, developers avoid quick fixes and "spaghetti code," leading to systems that remain maintainable over time. OOAD reduces long-term maintenance costs and prevents software degradation as projects evolve.

129. Evaluate how UML component diagrams assist in third-party API integrations.
Answer: UML component diagrams assist in third-party API integrations by visually representing how external APIs interact with system components. They highlight provided and required interfaces, making it easier to identify dependencies and plan integration points. For example, a payment gateway API can be modeled as a component with specific operations, clarifying how it connects with the core application. This visualization supports planning for security, error handling, and scalability in API usage. Component diagrams ensure seamless integration, reduce complexity, and aid in documenting external dependencies for future maintenance.

130. Explain how object-oriented design supports edge computing in IoT systems.
Answer: Object-oriented design supports edge computing in IoT systems by structuring software as modular components that can operate independently on edge devices. Encapsulation isolates sensor logic, data processing, and communication modules, enabling localized decision-making without reliance on centralized servers. Polymorphism supports diverse hardware and protocols, allowing flexible deployments across heterogeneous IoT devices. Design patterns like Strategy enable dynamic adaptation of data processing algorithms based on environmental conditions. This approach ensures that IoT systems remain responsive, scalable, and capable of operating efficiently in distributed, resource-constrained environments.

Printed at Repro India Ltd.